Susan

Creating Effective
Teams

A Guide for Members and Leaders

SAGE Publications
International Educational and Professional Publisher
Thousand Oaks   London   New Delhi

For information:

SAGE Publications, Inc.
2455 Teller Road
Thousand Oaks, California 91320
E-mail: order@sagepub.com

SAGE Publications Ltd.
6 Bonhill Street
London EC2A 4PU
United Kingdom

SAGE Publications India Pvt. Ltd.
M-32 Market
Greater Kailash I
New Delhi 110 048 India

Printed in the United States of America

Library of Congress Cataloging-in-Publication Data

Wheelan, Susan A.
    Creating effective teams: A guide for members and leaders / by
Susan A. Wheelan.
        p.   cm.
    Includes bibliographical references and index.
    ISBN 0-7619-1816-7 (cloth: alk. paper)
    ISBN 0-7619-1817-5 (pbk.: alk. paper)
    1. Teams in the workplace.   I. Title.
    HD66.W485   1999
    658.4'02—dc21   99-6224

                03   04   05   7   6   5

Acquiring Editor:	Marquita Flemming
Editorial Assistant:	MaryAnn Vail
Production Editor:	Denise Santoyo
Editorial Assistant:	Karen Wiley
Typesetter:	Marion Warren
Indexer:	Jeanne Busemeyer
Cover Designer:	Candice Harman

Contents

*To all the teams
and team members
who let me learn from them*

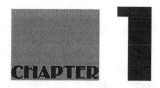

CHAPTER 1

Why Groups?

Groups Have a Long History of Success

People have formed work groups in order to accomplish goals and tasks since the beginning of human history. The small group, whose members work collaboratively for their mutual benefit or survival, is the oldest form of social organization. Groups have played a major role in both the survival of human beings and the development of human culture. Some would argue that our ability to work together was, and is, the key to human survival and advancement. Work groups have a long and remarkable track record of success. From the beginning of human history, people have utilized work groups to generate new ideas, get things done, and nurture individuals.

We Need Groups Every Day

The vast majority of people participate in work groups on a daily basis and have always done so. Imagine building a house or an airplane, putting out a newspaper, developing a strategic plan, or doing almost anything, all by yourself. Of course, there are tasks that can, or should, be done by one person, but given the complex nature of work as we enter the 21st century, more and more tasks require people to work in groups.

There was a period of time when we tried to get rid of the collaborative nature of work. We set up assembly lines and precisely defined each person's job so that he or she could do that job without input from others. Often, this was effective. The industrial revolution was a success, after all. But this strategy worked best for repetitive tasks where innovation, creativity, and problem solving were not necessary. As we approach the 21st century, there are fewer tasks like that left that humans perform. Robots have most of those jobs.

Even during the early industrial period, groups functioned all over the workplace. People made decisions together. Engineers created new products together. Managers determined schedules and hammered out work flow processes together. The need for work groups just didn't go away.

There's Too Much to Know

The current emphasis on work groups reflects our growing awareness that the complexity of work at this point in history requires collaboration. More work is conducted by groups of employees not for frivolous reasons but because it is the only way to accomplish tasks. Too much knowledge and too many different skills are required for any individual to accomplish such complex tasks successfully alone.

The knowledge explosion led us to reevaluate the way we work. The assembly line model has lost much of its relevance. The "individual contributor" no longer can go it alone. Teamwork is necessary for organizational success.

When Teams Are Good, They're Very, Very Good

Lots of people don't like to work in groups. Many of us don't like to go to meetings and think that they are a waste of time. Most of us have had some bad experiences working in groups. Some of us associate work groups with fighting, hurt feelings, and inefficiency. This is not surprising, since many groups have difficulty functioning effectively. Even groups that are ultimately successful have periods that are stressful and unpleasant.

Yet when a group becomes a team, there is nothing like it. Work doesn't feel like a chore. It's fun. Members of high performance teams feel involved, committed, and valued. Time flies, work flows, and people help each other to meet goals and deadlines. There's nothing like playing on a winning team. Effective teams are more productive, and that means that companies and organizations win, too. The trick is to learn enough about how work groups function so that we can increase the chances that work groups will become high performance teams.

The distinction between a work group and a team is an important one in this book. A work group is composed of members who are striving to create a shared view of goals and to develop an efficient and effective organizational structure in which to accomplish those goals. A work group becomes a team when shared goals have been established and effective methods to accomplish those goals are in place. How work groups become teams is what this book is about. It chronicles how some groups develop into high performance teams and why other groups fail to become teams. Throughout the book, I refer to work groups that are effective and productive as teams. Those that have not reached that level of effectiveness and productivity are referred to as work groups.

Creating Effective Teams

Books, articles, and research studies that attempt to describe the characteristics of high performance work teams have proliferated over the past few decades. The importance of teamwork in increasing organizational productivity is clear, and everyone has jumped on the bandwagon to ensure team success. Employees go to training sessions to learn how to work in teams. In some companies, employees wear T-shirts with their team name printed on the front. Teams often are provided with leaders, coaches, facilitators, and consultants. The intense focus on teams and team performance makes this feel new and faddish even though working together to get things done is as old as humanity itself.

While "teaming" may feel like a fad or a craze, it's not. Groups and teams have always been with us and will not go away. We can hope that some of the faddish trends in relation to teams will go away. The importance of teams in the workplace, however, is here to stay.

The bad news about the intense focus on work groups is that everyone is trying to develop methods to help groups become more effective and productive, and not everyone knows what they are doing. Strategies designed to increase group effectiveness have proliferated as more and more organizations have initiated programs such as team development, team building, and the like. Current team development strategies, however, range from the ridiculous to the sublime. (My personal favorite in the ridiculous category is a group of executives playing basketball while riding donkeys as a way to build a high performance team.) As a result, determining what to do to help groups perform effectively has become extremely difficult. What strategies work? What strategies are based on solid research evidence? What strategies are cost- and time effective? These and other similar questions are on the minds of many people charged with ensuring the effectiveness of organizational work groups. Answers, however, are not so easy to come by.

The good news about the intense focus on work groups is that it has rejuvenated the scientific study of work groups and high performance teams. We've learned a lot more about how groups develop and what makes them effective. Social scientists all over the world have returned to the study of groups. We don't know everything yet, but we know enough to begin to be helpful to people working in groups. We know enough to answer some of those difficult questions outlined earlier. That's what this book is about. The goal of this book is to translate what we've learned into straightforward, user-friendly, practical guidelines for members and leaders. It also will provide guidance for those who interact with a particular work group and for those who manage them.

How to Use This Book

This book grew out of a number of requests that I've had from organizational members to write a jargon-free "how to" book describing how work groups function and what to do to help work groups become high performance teams. While I'm not enamored of how-to books, I decided to try

---

BOX 1.1
Silly Team Building Activities

I've asked people over the years what was the silliest team building activity they've participated in. Here are some of my favorites:
- Introductions involving linking your name with a personality trait (e. g., Chatty Cathy, Serious Sam, Jumpy Jill)
- Rock climbing to increase profits
- Leading a blindfolded teammate around the block
- Anything that involves sharing feelings you don't want to share
- Creating a human sculpture out of your teammates
- Anything involving construction paper

---

my hand at this one because the topic is so important. I agreed to write this book on one condition, however. I'm not going to make anything up. Whatever I write will be based on research evidence and if I'm speculating, I'll let you know. I promise not to overwhelm you with references in the text; those references will appear at the end of the book. If you want more information, the references will be there for you.

I've included case examples throughout the book and a few things I've heard, witnessed, been told about, or asked people about over the years. These will appear in boxes like the one in this chapter. These anecdotes have helped me, and people I've worked with, to maintain a sense of humor and compassion about working in groups and teams. I hope you find them useful.

This book is meant to be used, not just read. I envision the members of newly formed groups reading the first six chapters and discussing them together as a way of getting off to a good start. Chapter 2 discusses what the larger organization can do to help groups be successful. Chapter 3 describes how groups develop and function. In Chapter 4, the characteristics of productive teams are outlined. This will help the members of a new group to know what they are shooting for. The characteristic of effective members and effective leaders are outlined in Chapters 5 and 6, respectively.

Talk with each other about what you've read. Use the information as a way to begin to organize your group. Use the book like you would a manual for a computer program. When you get stuck, refer to the appropriate chapter.

Once the group gets under way, refer to Chapter 7, which describes typical situations that arise in the first stage of group development. The chapter outlines ways that members and leaders can be helpful during this stage. Chapters 8 and 9 do the same thing for groups at Stage 2 and 3, respectively. Chapter 10 outlines how to maintain high performance at Stage 4.

Reading this book once won't be enough. Like other changes in attitudes or behaviors, learning to utilize this information in the work groups you belong to will take time. Attitudes and behaviors don't change overnight.

I bring about 25 years of experience with groups and teams to this project and I'm not bored yet. Studying groups and working with their members is endlessly fascinating and challenging. Beyond that, I believe that helping work groups become high performance teams is crucial not only to the bottom line but also to the creation of humane, interesting, diverse, and challenging workplaces. I hope this book furthers the achievement of those goals.

CHAPTER **2**

Effective Organizational Support for Teams

Some organizations have been very successful in making the shift to a team environment. Others have not done so well. This chapter outlines what we know from research and theory about the role of the organization in facilitating or inhibiting the development of high performance work teams. That role is quite large and very important, but it receives little organizational attention. The reason for this is simple. It seems easier to create work groups and focus our efforts on group results than to address organizational issues that may be inhibiting group performance. If organizations want effective teams, however, then all organization members, especially upper management, should consider the following guidelines.

Plant Groups in a Favorable Organizational Climate

Work groups and teams function better in an organizational culture that:

- Clearly defines the organizational mission
- Supports innovation

7

- Expects success
- Values superior quality and service
- Pays attention to detail
- Values team recommendations
- Sets clear expectations for group output, quality, timing, and pacing
- Rewards teamwork rather than individual performance

— Clearly Defines the Organizational Mission

Groups flourish when members are clear about what business they are in. This may seem obvious, but it is not always so. Once I asked a group what the mission of its organization was and the members did not know, despite the fact that the organization's mission statement was clearly displayed on the wall of the group's meeting room. In another case, I asked a group what its organization's mission was and the members sang the mission statement! Their singing was not sweet or lyrical. It was done in that singsong way that expresses derision and disrespect. Organization members not only need to know the words contained in the mission statement, they also need to understand and believe those words.

— Supports Innovation

Some organizations tend to do things the way they've always been done. If this is the case, or if organization members believe that this is the case, groups will have more difficulty being successful. When you put a group of people together, the combined intelligence and creativity of group members often lead to new and unexpected ideas and solutions. If the group is functioning in an organization that encourages new ideas and new ways of doing things, members feel energized and supported. If not, members quickly become dispirited and begin to believe that there is no point to making suggestions that challenge the status quo.

— Expects Success

Some organizations don't expect to be successful. This may sound absurd, but there are many examples of this attitude expressed in different ways by organization members. Here are just a few.

"What do you expect? This is a government agency."

"The CEO is leaving soon and doesn't really care about what we do."

"We're going to be merged anyway."

"People would rather be safe than successful."

If attitudes such as these exist in an organizational culture, group members will not give their best effort because they believe that giving 100% is not encouraged or valued.

— Values Superior Quality and Service

In the real world, there is always some tension between quality, service, and profit. If, however, organization members perceive that profit is more important than quality or service, they also will become dispirited and cynical. Some examples of how this gets expressed are listed next.

"People care more about their stock options than doing a good job."

"They want us to pretend to be working to keep the inspectors off our backs."

"They talk about customer service, but they don't really mean it."

— Pays Attention to Detail

"Get a group together and work out this policy issue" is an example of lack of attention to detail. The alternative would be a clear definition of the group's task; the provision of all backup materials; and awareness and preplanning about group membership, time lines, meeting times, workloads, availability of potential members, and the like.

— Values Team Recommendations

If group members believe that whatever they come up with will be rejected or changed by upper management, the chances of group success are considerably diminished. If group leaders are told in advance what the group should come up with, success is even more unlikely. Again, this is self-evident, but, unfortunately, examples such as these are all too common. In such an environment, groups are used so that the organization seems to be seeking member input when, in fact, it is not.

— Sets Clear Expectations for Group Output, Quality, Timing, and Pacing

If the group is given realistic guidelines and goals for what members are expected to produce and by when, the chances of success are greatly increased. For example, it is unrealistic to give a group 2 months to complete a complex task, especially if members of that group have not worked together as a group in the past. It also is unrealistic to give a group a long-term project without some way of measuring progress along the way.

— Rewards Teamwork Rather Than Individual Performance

Rewarding teamwork rather than individual performance is one of the most difficult issues that organizations face with regard to setting up work groups. Most compensation systems are designed to evaluate and reward individual contributions, not team contributions. If individuals are to be motivated to work to create a high performance team, however, then the team's performance should be the determinant of compensation and bonuses.

Team compensation systems are discussed and written about quite a lot. However, most organizations do not have team compensation systems in place. In fact, in many cases, members of teams from different areas of a company actually may be hurting the bottom line of their area by participating on a cross-functional team. Situations such as these hurt overall team performance.

Some organizations use recognition of team performance as a substitute for financial reward. Although this is helpful in some cases, the type of recognition has to be carefully thought out. Sometimes recognition of one team may create competition among teams. This can inhibit performance because most teams rely on cooperation from other teams to accomplish their goals. In other cases, the kind of recognition can be a source of embarrassment to some team members.

Team compensation strategies are sorely needed. I wish I could recommend an approach. However, there has been insufficient experimentation with team compensation to have any sense of what works well and what doesn't.

Give Groups What They Need to Do Their Best

Work groups function better in organizations that:

- Establish meaningful group goals and meaningful tasks that require skill, have variety, and require interdependence in order to accomplish those goals and tasks
- Establish meaningful group goals and tasks that require continuous learning
- Establish access to the technical resources necessary to accomplish tasks
- Establish access to the human resources necessary to accomplish group goals
- Establish defined team work areas

— Establish Meaningful Group Goals and Meaningful Tasks

Group members function better when they feel that group goals and tasks are meaningful, interesting, and challenge them to think and work to capacity. If tasks are seen as routine or boring, motivation is diminished. Of course, many organizational tasks are routine or boring but still must be done. A team format may not be the best way to accomplish those tasks.

Group goals and tasks also should require interdependence. That is, a team should be necessary to accomplish them. Again, this seems self-evident, but a few examples will make it obvious that many groups have goals and tasks that do not require members to work together. They are treated as teams but, in fact, are not teams. Examples include:

- Phone solicitors who work independently but are called a team and meet once a week to discuss team performance
- Salespeople who work independently, are paid for individual sales, and meet once a month to discuss team performance
- The top 50 administrators in an organization who meet monthly to hear a report from the CEO
- People who report to the same boss but don't interact with each other at any other time

— **Establish Meaningful Group Goals and Tasks
That Require Continuous Learning**

Groups with goals and tasks that require continuous learning are more
successful. The best thing about a group is that, if it has the right goals and
tasks, members will learn from each other and will seek out information
to learn more about how to proceed. If the goals and tasks don't require
new learning, a group format is probably not necessary for their accomplishment.

— **Establish Access to the Technical Resources
Necessary to Accomplish Tasks**

You can't build a house without tools. Yet many teams are expected to
accomplish tasks without even minimal access to computer equipment, fax
machines, computer programs, archival materials, and other resources
necessary for goal achievement.

— **Establish Access to the Human Resources
Necessary to Accomplish Group Goals**

A group that is expected to produce a new product on time and under
budget but with no authority over, or access to, the people who set production schedules will not be successful. A group that is expected to determine best practices in a certain area but has no budget to visit other organizations or to consult experts in the area will in all likelihood be
unsuccessful. A group mired in conflict and that cannot ask for assistance
from an internal or external consultant to help them work out their differences also will have great difficulty being successful.

— **Establish Defined Team Work Areas**

A group needs a territory. This has become increasingly difficult because, in larger organizations, group members may be spread out over
large geographical areas. While e-mail and teleconferencing can help to
some extent, groups do better when they have regular face-to-face meet-

---

BOX 2.1
Old English

The boss asked, "What are you guys going to need to do your best work?" A team member replied, "A work space with more modern equipment than Dickens used would be helpful."

---

ings. If distance prohibits frequent meetings, the meetings that do occur should be long enough to allow for extended planning, discussions, and decision making. For groups in the same geographic location, a defined work area is very useful. Proximity makes communication easier, and the work progresses faster. We are, after all, still human. We need to know the people in our group. We don't need to know other members intimately, but we do need to know people's thoughts and attitudes about the work that we are doing together.

Pick Members Based on Their Ability to Do the Task and Their Ability to Contribute to Group Success

There's a lot more research about leaders than members. Literally thousands of studies have been done to determine what makes a good leader. Very little has been done to determine what makes a good group member. Even with all the attention paid to leadership, we still don't know very much. In the case of members, we know even less.

What is known about effective members is discussed in more detail in Chapter 5. By way of a preview, however, I can say that the research literature does not conclude that personality assessments of potential group members or that the personality or style compatibility of group members are key to group success. Rather, it suggests that members knowledgeable about how groups operate and knowledgeable about the group's tasks are best.

In addition, the research literature does not suggest that members have to like each other or socialize outside of work in order for groups to be successful. Instead, it suggests that people trained in the technical aspects of the job, in how groups function, and in what members and leaders can do to help groups function more effectively make good group members. Organizations that focus on educating and training people about the technical aspects of their job and about effective group participation will increase the likelihood that organizational groups will become high performance teams.

Educate People for Group Participation Competence

As was just stated, organizations that focus on educating and training people about the technical aspects of their job and about effective group participation will increase the likelihood that organizational groups will become high performance teams.

Most organizations do a reasonable job of choosing people with technical expertise and providing ongoing technical training to their employees. When it comes to group participation of members or leaders, however, organizations don't do so well. Most employees in large organizations have attended the obligatory half-day workshop on group dynamics and many have attended leadership training or team development workshops. However, the quality and duration of these experiences vary widely.

Imagine providing computer training that was inaccurate or incomplete. Imagine giving technicians inaccurate information about turbine maintenance. While I'm sure that this happens occasionally, organizations tend to be careful and conservative about technical training. Unfortunately, this is not the case with group or leadership training. Organizations forget to ask training providers some very basic and important questions. These questions are:

1. What is taught in this training?
2. Is the content of the training based on solid research evidence?
3. Can the trainer provide us with social science references regarding the training content?

BOX 2.2
Looking Good

As part of a class assignment, some of my students surveyed companies, asking how they selected outside trainers to conduct team-building workshops. The most frequent response was that the trainer's brochure and materials (overheads, manuals, etc.) had to be of the highest professional quality. References are rarely checked.

---

4. Does the training work? Do people who attend this training actually perform better as group members or leaders?

By the way, these questions do not have easy answers, and training providers should not be expected to be able to answer each question completely. All training providers should be able to answer the first three pretty well, however. There may be other literature that disagrees with the provider's conclusions, but he or she should be aware of a body of literature that supports the content of his or her training. If the trainer is unable to answer the first three questions, head for the hills.

With regard to the fourth question, there has been insufficient investigation of this question to answer it with any certainty. Whether people who attend group dynamics or leadership training actually perform better as group members or leaders remains an open question. Do not despair, however. Establish internal studies to address this question. Collaborate with external research experts and internal human resource and organizational development specialists to explore this question. A great deal of money is spent on these kinds of training, and, in my opinion, much of that money is wasted.

Avoid Unsubstantiated Team Development and Consultation Strategies

Since not all work groups manage to reach high levels of effectiveness and productivity on their own, efforts to develop intervention strategies that will assist groups in meeting goals and maximizing effectiveness have been employed for many years. Unfortunately, most team interventions don't work. Sundstrom, DeMeuse, and Futrell, for example, examined a number of intervention studies and noted that in four of the nine interventions that measured group performance, the interventions had positive effects on group performance. That means that in five of the nine, performance was unchanged. Interventions have had mixed results, at best, on group effectiveness and productivity.

Guzzo, Jett, and Katzell conducted an analysis of 330 group intervention studies. They found that interventions that included goal setting and feedback had the most positive effects on group productivity. Interventions that take group development into account also are useful, since groups need different types of interventions at different points in their development.

To date, the most promising intervention type appears to be goal setting combined with feedback that includes attention to group development issues. The likely reason for the effectiveness of this combined intervention type is that group members set the goals and determine the strategies for improvement themselves. In short, group members and leaders are active as opposed to passive participants in the intervention process. Also, this type of intervention is tailored to meet the needs of a group at a particular point in time. It does not assume that one intervention type fits all groups.

Needless to say, research does not suggest that rock climbing, whitewater rafting, blind trust walks, or playing basketball on donkeys increases productivity in any way. These kinds of activities are fun for some people and distasteful to others. In any case, there is no evidence that they facilitate changes in group effectiveness or productivity.

Before choosing an intervention to facilitate group performance, questions should be asked as well. These are:

1. What are the underlying assumptions of the intervention? That is, how will the intervention change the dynamics of the group?
2. Is the intervention based on solid research evidence?
3. Can the consultant provide us with social science references regarding the intervention?

4. Does the intervention work? Do work groups that participate in this type of intervention increase their effectiveness and productivity?

As was the case with training approaches, if the consultant cannot answer the first three questions, head for the hills. Also, head for the hills if the consultant bases his or her response solely on personal experience. The good news is that there is research available to answer the fourth question. Although more research is needed, we can say that interventions that include goal setting, performance feedback, and attention to group development issues work better than other approaches. Until we learn more, it is best to employ interventions that contain these three elements.

Avoid Helping Groups Too Much

Many groups are getting too much help. They often have an array of helpers such as sponsors, coaches, leaders, trainers, and consultants. Help, however, is not always helpful. Throughout this chapter I have outlined things that groups really need and what they need when they get stuck. I have found no evidence in the literature that increasing the number of expert helpers who meet with the team on a regular basis has any positive effects.

When groups ask for help, give it to them, but make sure that the help conforms to the guidelines outlined earlier in this chapter. Too much help often increases group dependency on experts and reduces the chances that members will learn to be effective and productive on their own.

I mentioned this briefly in a previous section, but I reiterate it here because it is so important: Groups need accurate and frequent feedback about their performance. Without feedback, it is very difficult to judge progress or make corrections to get back on course. Some groups get lots of feedback. Others get almost none. Research tells us that those that get feedback regularly will be more successful.

Make Sure That Each Group Has Enough Autonomy to Do Its Work But Remains Connected With the Rest of the Organization

The mission of every group should be clear to other organizational groups and individuals. If organization members and units are expected to help each other, they must know what others are doing.

Groups also need sufficient autonomy to do their work. They need to be clear about what decisions they can make and what decisions need to be reviewed by others. At the same time, groups must stay in close contact with other organizational members and groups. If an isolated group makes a decision without involving others in that decision, the odds of having that decision countermanded or ignored increase significantly. Effective relationships with other organization members and groups are important indicators of an effective team.

Conduct Organizational Support Reviews Regularly

Many of the guidelines outlined in this chapter could be read as things that only upper management can accomplish. It is not my intention to imply that. Every member of the organization has a role to play in the success of groups with which that member interacts. Each group has a responsibility to solicit the things necessary for its success as well.

Before and during the life of any group, it would be helpful to review these guidelines to determine the level of organizational support and to make changes as needed. Group members, or potential members, along with others external to the group who interact with that group in some meaningful way, should conduct these reviews. Periodic review sessions focused on organizational support, not group performance, will have at least two effects. First, problems with the level of organizational support can be identified and corrected early. Second, group members will be encouraged by the efforts of others to ensure that the group becomes a high performance team.

The idea of organizational support review sessions has not been researched. It is based on research, however. That is, because research has outlined a number of organizational factors that increase the chances of group success, it is only logical that organization members attempt to ensure that these factors are being addressed.

The following checklist is provided to help people participating in an organizational support review session evaluate the level of organizational support for a particular group. Participants should complete the checklist anonymously prior to the meeting. Ensuring individual anonymity is crucial to the success of this process. Individuals must feel free to be candid in their responses.

A summary should be prepared prior to the meeting as well. At the meeting, participants should discuss the summary and identify areas where organizational support is adequate or superior and areas that need improvement. Action steps should be outlined as well. There will be areas where, for legitimate reasons, support cannot be provided at ideal levels. Aim to do the best you can.

The Organizational Support Checklist

Organization Name _____

Business/Division, Area Name _____

Group ID Number _____

Member ID Number_____

Date _____

Group Size _____

Please read the statements below. Circle the number that most accurately describes your response to the statement. Use the following key to respond to each statement.

> 1. **disagree strongly**
> 2. **disagree to some extent**
> 3. **agree to some extent**
> 4. **agree strongly**

1. This organization has a clearly defined organizational mission.

1   2   3   4

2. This organization supports innovation.

1   2   3   4

3. This organization expects to be successful.

$$1 \quad 2 \quad 3 \quad 4$$

4. This organization values superior quality in all work endeavors.

$$1 \quad 2 \quad 3 \quad 4$$

5. Organization members pay attention to detail.

$$1 \quad 2 \quad 3 \quad 4$$

6. This organization values team recommendations.

$$1 \quad 2 \quad 3 \quad 4$$

7. This organization has clear expectations about the quality of our group's output.

$$1 \quad 2 \quad 3 \quad 4$$

8. This organization has clear expectations for our group's timing.

$$1 \quad 2 \quad 3 \quad 4$$

9. The goals of our group are meaningful.

$$1 \quad 2 \quad 3 \quad 4$$

10. The tasks of our group are interesting to members.

$$1 \quad 2 \quad 3 \quad 4$$

11. The tasks of our group require members to work collaboratively.

$$1 \quad 2 \quad 3 \quad 4$$

12. The tasks of our group require continuous learning.

$$1 \quad 2 \quad 3 \quad 4$$

13. Our group has access to the technical resources necessary to accomplish tasks.

$$1 \quad 2 \quad 3 \quad 4$$

14. Our group has access to the human resources necessary to accomplish group tasks.

$$1 \quad 2 \quad 3 \quad 4$$

15. Our group has a defined work area.

$$1 \quad 2 \quad 3 \quad 4$$

16. Our group receives regular feedback about its performance and progress.

1   2   3   4

17. Our group receives positive recognition for group achievements.

1   2   3   4

18. Financial rewards are based on group achievements.

1   2   3   4

19. Our group was provided with members with appropriate technical skills.

1   2   3   4

20. Our group was provided with members with skills in the area of group participation.

1   2   3   4

21. Our group was provided a leader with skills in the area of group management and participation.

1   2   3   4

22. Our group has been provided with all technical training necessary for group success.

1   2   3   4

23. Our group has been provided with appropriate group dynamics training.

1   2   3   4

24. Our group leader has been provided with appropriate leadership training.

1   2   3   4

25. Our group has been provided with consultant help deemed necessary for group success.

1   2   3   4

26. Our group's goals are clear to the rest of the organization.

1   2   3   4

27. Our group has sufficient autonomy to do its work.

1   2   3   4

28. Our group is in close communication with appropriate organizational members and groups.

1   2   3   4

If group training was provided, please answer the following questions:

29. I learned what I needed to know to work successfully with this group.

1   2   3   4

30. I felt that the trainer(s) were competent.

1   2   3   4

If group consultation was provided, please answer the following questions:

31. The consultation helped the group to work more effectively together.

1   2   3   4

32. I felt that the consultant(s) were competent.

1   2   3   4

Minimum Score: 28

Maximum Score: 128

My Score:_____

CHAPTER 3

From Groups to Teams:

The Stages of Group Development

Groups develop across time very much like people do. People experience childhood, adolescence, young adulthood, adulthood, and old age. Childhood is associated with dependency. Adolescence usually contains some periods of conflict. Young adults spend a lot of time developing trusting relationships and preparing for work careers. Adults spend a significant amount of time working, and older adults typically begin reducing their focus on work. Research has found that groups also experience periods of dependency, conflict, trust and structuring, work, and disengagement. Group development and human development have much in common.

The concept of group development is well documented in the social science literature. In view of the general consensus that groups develop and change across time, extensive reviews of the literature have been conducted in order to consolidate previous research and to propose a unified model of group development. These reviews have produced similar results. What follows is a brief description of the integrated model of group development that I use in my own work. The integrated model of group development initially was based on previous research. Since then, a number of studies have been conducted to determine whether these stages actually occurred in work groups. To date, these studies have supported the fact that the stages of development outlined in the model do occur in real-world groups.

Stage 1: Dependency and Inclusion

The first stage of group development is characterized by member dependency on the designated leader, concerns about safety, and concerns about feeling included. This first stage of group development may manifest itself as compliance with plans proposed by the group leader or by a powerful member. Group members often engage in what has been called pseudo-work, or flight, such as exchanging stories about customers or their families that not relevant to the task at hand. Members also may wait for the group leader to make decisions. In fact, members often urge the leader to take charge and tell them what to do. Members seem more concerned with being accepted by others than with the task at hand. They are unlikely to express different points of view as a result. Stage 1 groups have the following characteristics:

Identifying a Stage 1 Group

1. Members are concerned with personal safety in the group.
2. Members are concerned with acceptance and inclusion by others in the group.
3. Members fear rejection.
4. Members communicate in tentative and very polite ways.
5. Members express a need for dependable and directive leadership.
6. The leader is seen as benevolent and competent.
7. The leader is expected and encouraged to provide members with direction and personal safety.
8. The leader is very rarely challenged.
9. Goals are not clear to members, but clarification is not sought.
10. Members rarely express disagreement with initial group goals.
11. The group assumes that consensus about goals exists.

```
┌─────────────────────────────────────────────────────────────────┐
│                                                                   │
│                           BOX 3.1                                 │
│                      Silence of the Lambs                         │
│                                                                   │
│   You know you're in a Stage 1 group when the leader asks a       │
│   question and no one responds. The leader's words seem to vanish │
│   into the Bermuda Triangle.                                      │
│                                                                   │
└─────────────────────────────────────────────────────────────────┘
```

12. Role assignments tend to be based on external status, first impressions, and initial self-presentation rather than matching member competencies with goal and task requirements.
13. Member compliance is high.
14. Communication tends to go through the leader.
15. Participation is generally limited to a few vocal members.
16. Conflict is minimal.
17. Conformity is high.
18. A lack of group structure and organization is evident.
19. Member deviation from emerging norms is rare.
20. Cohesion and commitment to the group is based on identification with the leader.
21. Subgroups and coalitions are rare at this stage.

Stage 2: Counterdependency and Fight

At Stage 2, the group seeks to free itself from its dependence on the leader and members fight among themselves about group goals and procedures. Conflict is an inevitable part of this process. The group's task at this stage is to develop a unified set of goals, values, and operational procedures, and this task usually generates conflict. Conflict is also necessary for the establishment of trust and a climate in which members feel free to disagree with each other.

Some groups become mired in conflict and remain stuck at this developmental stage. Other groups are overwhelmed by the stress of this phase and revert to leader dependence in an attempt to avoid further conflict.

BOX 3.2
Wolves in Sheep's Clothing?

You know you're in a Stage 2 group when you'd rather have all your teeth pulled than go to the next meeting.

Neither outcome has positive effects for the group or for the quality of work generated by the group. Only through conflict resolution and the development of a unified view of the group's purpose and processes can true collaboration be achieved.

Identifying a Stage 2 Group

1. Conflicts about values emerge.
2. Disagreements about goals and tasks emerge.
3. Increased feelings of safety allow dissent to occur.
4. Dissatisfaction with roles may surface.
5. Clarification of goals begins.
6. Role clarification also begins.
7. Members challenge the leader and each other.
8. Subgroups and coalitions form.
9. Group intolerance of subgroups, cliques, and coalitions is evident.
10. Increased member participation is evident.
11. Decreased conformity begins.
12. Deviation from emerging group norms begins to occur.
13. Attempts at conflict management begin.
14. If efforts to resolve conflicts are successful, increased consensus about group goals and culture become evident near the end of this stage.
15. Conflict resolution, if successful, increases trust and cohesion.

Stage 3: Trust and Structure

If a group manages to work through the inevitable conflicts of Stage 2, member trust, commitment to the group, and willingness to cooperate in-

---

BOX 3.3
How He's Changed!

You know you're in a Stage 3 group when the group member who drove you crazy for weeks begins to make you smile.

---

crease. Communication becomes more open and task oriented. Professional territoriality decreases as members focus more on the task and less on issues of status, power, or influence. This third stage of group development is characterized by more mature negotiations about roles, organization, and procedures. It is also a time in which members work to solidify positive working relationships with each other.

Identifying a Stage 3 Group

1. Increased goal clarity and consensus are evident.
2. Roles and tasks are adjusted to increase the likelihood of goal achievement.
3. The leader's role becomes less directive and more consultative.
4. The communication structure becomes more flexible.
5. The content of communication becomes more task oriented.
6. Pressures to conform increase again.
7. Helpful deviation is tolerated.
8. Coalitions and subgroups continue to occur.
9. Increased tolerance of subgroups, cliques, and coalitions is evident.
10. Cohesion and trust increase.
11. Member satisfaction also increases.
12. Cooperation is more evident.
13. Individual commitment to group goals and tasks is high.
14. Greater division of labor occurs.
15. Conflict continues to occur but it is managed more effectively.
16. The group works to clarify and build a group structure that will facilitate goal achievement.

Stage 4: Work

As its name implies, the fourth stage of group development is a time of intense team productivity and effectiveness. At this stage the group becomes a high performance team. Having resolved many of the issues of the previous stages, the team can focus more of its energy on goal achievement and task accomplishment. Although some work occurs at every developmental stage, the quality and quantity of work increases significantly during Stage 4.

Identifying a Stage 4 Group

1. Members are clear about team goals.
2. Members agree with the team's goals.
3. Tasks are appropriate to team versus individual solution.
4. Members are clear about their roles.
5. Members accept their roles and status in the team.
6. Role assignments match member abilities.
7. During the work stage, delegation or "unleadership" is the prevailing leadership style.
8. The team's communication structure matches the demands of the task.
9. The team has an open communication structure in which all members participate and are heard.
10. The team has an appropriate ratio of task and supportive communications.
11. The team gets, gives, and utilizes feedback about its effectiveness and productivity.
12. The team spends time defining problems it must solve or decisions it must make.
13. The team spends time planning how it will solve problems and make decisions.
14. The team spends enough time discussing problems and decisions that must be solved.
15. The team determines methods for decision making that are participatory.

BOX 3.4
In the Zone

You know you're in a Stage 4 group when being on the team makes you feel better than Prozac.

---

16. The team implements and evaluates its solutions and decisions.
17. Voluntary conformity is high.
18. Task-related deviance is tolerated.
19. Team norms encourage high performance and quality.
20. The team expects to be successful.
21. The team encourages innovation.
22. Team members pay attention to the details of their work.
23. The team accepts coalition and subgroup formation.
24. Subgroups are integrated into the team-as-a-whole.
25. Subgroups work on important tasks.
26. Tasks contain variety and challenge.
27. Subgroups work on a total product or project.
28. The team contains the smallest number of members necessary to accomplish its goals.
29. Subgroups are recognized and rewarded by the team.
30. The team is highly cohesive.
31. Interpersonal attraction among members is high.
32. Members are cooperative.
33. Periods of conflict are frequent but brief.
34. The team has effective conflict management strategies.

Group development does not always proceed in a positive direction. Groups can get stuck at a particular stage for extended periods of time, resulting in long-term ineffectiveness and low productivity. Also, groups may fluctuate widely based on the circumstances and forces affecting them at a given moment. Changes in membership, external demands, and changes in leadership can all affect the work of a group. Turnover rates, reassignments, and new upper-level managers often produce regression and require rebuilding of group structures and culture.

BOX 3.5
The Stages of Group Development

    I.   Dependency and Inclusion
   II.   Counterdependence and Fight
  III.   Trust and Structure
  IV.   Work and Productivity

Not all groups, of any type, achieve adequate levels of effectiveness and productivity. In fact, some studies estimate that between 80% and 90% of all groups have difficulties with performance. While achieving effective performance levels is difficult for any group, it is even more problematic for groups with diverse members. Groups composed of members from different professions, for example, have additional obstacles to productivity. These include the lack of an organizing framework, issues of professional territoriality, and miscommunication. The road to productivity is fraught with difficulties.

Surviving Group Development

Based on what has been discussed so far, there are a few things that people can do and a few attitudes that people can take on that make the process of group development easier. Like human development, groups have some rocky times on the road to maturity. Here are a few suggestions about how to survive, and even enjoy, the process of group development.

- *Learn about group development.*

It helps to know what's in store for you as you move through the various stages of individual human development. For example, once social scientists determined that adults experience developmental stages, some of which are not so pleasant, we all breathed a sigh of relief. Once we started talking about midlife crises, adolescent insecurities, menopause, and the like, many people stopped feeling alone and out of control. Instead of feeling scared or depressed, people felt normal. Other people were experiencing the same things and that made individuals feel better. It also makes the experiences of a particular age seem more manageable. Finally, it usually leads to a better, happier result.

The same is true of group development. If you know that all groups go through predictable stages of development, then you can relax and enjoy the ride. If you don't know about group development, you might think that your fellow group members are strange or that your particular group is extremely dysfunctional or unusual. The other good thing about knowledge of group behavior is that it will make you a better member or leader. You are less likely to misinterpret what you see and more likely to be able to be constructive in what you say and do.

- *Be patient.*

The good news is that while human development and group development have a lot in common, group development doesn't take as long. No one knows for sure how long it takes a typical group to get to Stage 4, but we do have a pretty good guess. My colleagues and I have been monitoring the progress of hundreds of groups over the years and we have yet to see a high performance team that had been meeting for less than 6 months. For the first 2 to 3 months, groups are dealing with issues characteristic of Stages 1 and 2. Stage 3 emerges in the fourth or fifth month, and Stage 4, or high performance, typically begins during the sixth or seventh month. Of course, this assumes that a group does not run into any snags.

The bad news about group development is that most people want groups to be functioning at high levels from the beginning. That simply doesn't happen. It takes time to figure out what goals really mean. It takes time to figure out how to accomplish those goals and who should do what. It takes time to resolve problems and disagreements that come up. Be patient.

The second bit of bad news is that some groups, like some people, never mature. They stay stuck in dependency or conflict for as long as the group exists. Other groups manage to become high performance teams only to regress to earlier stages. This is usually due to some internal crisis or change in the level of organizational support.

Fortunately, there is one more piece of good news. No group has to stay stuck or regressed. If members are willing to work to turn things around, it can be done.

- *Expect things to be murky at the beginning of a group.*

Things are never clear at the beginning of a group. Often, after an early meeting, you'll hear people asking each other questions about what went on during the meeting. Of course, no one asked those questions during the meeting. This is normal and, as time goes on, people will begin to feel free to ask for clarification during group meetings. If you expect a perfectly organized meeting with perfectly clear outcomes in a new group, you will be disappointed. You might even get angry, and that will do no one any good.

- *Expect conflict and treat it as a positive sign of progress.*

Most of us avoid conflict as much as we can. The problem in groups, as in life, is that conflict is inevitable. Each group has to define its goals, clarify how it will function, and determine the various roles that members will play. In addition, there will be disagreements about the content of the group's goal and how to solve specific problems related to that goal. Conflict is a necessary part of this process because, from divergent points of view, one relatively unified direction must be agreed upon if group members are to work together in a productive way.

On a more psychological level, conflict is necessary for the establishment of a safe environment. While, at first glance, this may seem paradoxical, conflict is helpful to the development of trust. We know, from our own experience, that it is easier to develop trust in another person or in a group if we believe that we can disagree and we won't be abandoned or hurt for our different perspective. It is difficult to trust those who deny us the right to be ourselves. Thus, marriages become more solid and real after the first fight. The same could be said of all human relationships. To engage in conflict with others and to "work it out" is an exhilarating experience. It provides energy, a commonly shared experience, a sense of safety and authenticity, and allows for deeper trust levels and collaboration.

From the task perspective, if people are not free to express their points of view, the group's product is likely to be an inferior one. If everyone just goes along with the first idea that's expressed, the outcome is unlikely to be of high quality. Conflict is a normal, natural, and necessary part of group life. Keeping that in mind will make things much easier.

- *Help the group to limit conflicts to those about tasks, roles, structures and the like. Don't get involved in personal feuds or personality conflicts.*

Although conflict may be normal and necessary, there are some kinds of conflict that can be very detrimental to group development. Personal feuds and personality conflicts that erupt in groups can cause group progress to cease, sometimes permanently. The problem with personal conflicts is that they usually can't be solved. If someone doesn't like another's personality, what can the rest of the group do about that? Often, personality conflicts really are the result of other factors in the group that can be addressed, such as goal confusion, role assignments, and the like. The group can deal with these things more successfully. In general, it's good to disagree about goals, tasks, roles, and the like. It is not good to personalize these things and see another member as bad or incompetent because he or she has a different opinion or a different way of doing things.

- *Compromise on issues when you can and help others to resolve differences.*

In the course of my research I have attended, or listened to tapes of, many group meetings. Sometimes, members are disagreeing and no one is willing to compromise. While I would not advocate compromise on an issue that is really important to group success or that has ethical consequences, compromise is essential to group productivity.

One example of an unwillingness to compromise always sticks out in my mind. The group was working on a very important new product for the company. The company had recently had a layoff, and more layoffs were anticipated. The group was over budget and had missed several deadlines. During my observation, a conflict unrelated to the goal of the group kept emerging. Members had taken sides on this issue, and neither side was willing to give in. This story has a happy ending. I worked with the group and helped them to see that this conflict about who was right would ultimately result in group failure. Most stories like this don't have happy endings.

- *Don't sit on the sidelines. Take responsibility for what is going on, even if it doesn't involve you directly.*

Every group member has responsibility for group outcomes. Don't wait for other members or the leader to solve a problem or save the day. Make suggestions. Share your ideas, concerns, and hesitations. Of course, it helps if you can do this in a diplomatic way.

- *Be supportive of other members and the leader.*

Some of the research that my colleagues and I have conducted over the years has required us to categorize each verbal statement made by group members into one of a number of categories. There is a category for supportive statements. Examples of these kinds of statements are:

"Thanks for that suggestion, Joe."
"I appreciate you saying that, Mary."
"I agree with you, Abe."

In groups that are doing well, out of every 100 statements made by group members, between 15 and 20 are supportive statements. That sounds like a lot, but we see this over and over again. There's nothing like a little support to encourage people to work to capacity.

- *Complete tasks that you accept or are given in a timely fashion.*

Groups are not just groups during meeting times. Members work together or separately outside of the group to complete work related to the group's goals. Nothing slows down group progress more than when those tasks are not accomplished in a timely fashion. Trust is built among members not by words but by actions. If we can trust each other to do what we say, things go very smoothly.

- *Don't be upset when subgroups or coalitions emerge.*

In order to get work done, subgroups are needed. In order to get a point across, we sometimes form a coalition with others to emphasize that point. These are natural and good things. Subgroups and coalitions upset some people. They may feel left out or believe that the presence of smaller units within the group will interfere with group success. Some people call these subgroups "cliques," which has negative connotations.

Relax. The presence of subgroups is a sign that the group is getting organized and will be able to get its work done during the inevitable crunch time. Coalitions can help the group to see another point of view, which, often, turns out to be the right one.

Of course, subgroups and coalitions can have negative effects sometimes. When coalitions are unwilling to compromise, for example, things can go awry. When subgroups take action without checking with or informing the whole group, the results can be negative. In general, however, the appearance of subgroups and coalitions is a healthy sign of group progress.

- *Encourage group members to assess how the group is functioning on a regular basis.*

People at work these days are very busy. We want the meeting to end quickly so that we can deal with the pile of work on our desk. The last thing we want to do is take 5 minutes out of the meeting to discuss how we are working together. The very last thing we want to do is spend an entire meeting every 2 months or so discussing how the group is functioning. That seems like a big waste of time. I encourage you to do it anyway. In the long run, it will save time and aggravation. More on how to assess group progress regularly can be found in Chapter 10.

- *Show up.*

I once worked with a group where the membership changed almost weekly. There were 20 people in this planning group. Each week about 10 people showed up, and those 10 were different almost every time. There is nothing like an unstable membership to slow group development or to stop it altogether. Each meeting becomes a repeat of the last, where the focus becomes catching people up on what happened at the last meeting.

In later chapters, I will offer more suggestions for members and leaders about what they can do to help their groups be successful. These were just for openers.

CHAPTER 4

How Do High Performance Teams Function?

S ome people I've come across think that all this focus on team development is a waste of time. They ask if any of this effort makes a difference to the bottom line. They are usually very surprised when I tell them that it does.

People are right to be skeptical about lots of the things currently being done to increase team effectiveness and productivity. Many of those things actually are a waste of time. There are things that high performance teams do, however, that make a very real difference to the bottom line.

Research studies on the relationship between internal team processes and productivity have identified a number of characteristics of high performance teams that are associated with productivity. These are listed next.

The Characteristics of High Performance Teams

- Members are clear about and agree with team goals.
- Tasks are appropriate to team versus individual solution.
- Members are clear about and accept their roles.
- Role assignments match member abilities.
- The leadership style matches the team's developmental level.

BOX 4.1
Tough Guys Don't Like Team Training

I was working with a group of hard hats. At first, they were pretty resistant to the training, which they referred to as "charm school." Finally, they were forced to admit that the group was functioning better. They decided that I was pretty cool for a "lady."

- An open communication structure allows all members to participate.
- The team gets, gives, and utilizes feedback about its effectiveness and productivity.
- The team spends time defining and discussing problems it must solve or decisions it must make.
- Members also spend time planning how they will solve problems and make decisions.
- The team uses effective decision-making strategies.
- The team implements and evaluates its solutions and decisions.
- Task-related deviance is tolerated.
- Team norms encourage high performance, quality, success, and innovation.
- Subgroups are integrated into the team-as-a-whole.
- The team contains the smallest number of members necessary to accomplish its goals.
- The team has sufficient time together to develop a mature working unit and to accomplish its goals.
- The team is highly cohesive and cooperative.
- Periods of conflict are frequent but brief, and the group has effective conflict management strategies.

Ten Keys to Productivity

The previous list of the characteristics of high performance teams suggests that there are 10 key areas that members should pay attention to in order to ensure the productivity of their group. Each of these areas is discussed next.

— 1. Goals

The most important characteristic of a high performance team is that its members are *clear about team goals.* Although this seems obvious, I have seen too many groups in which this was not the case. Even if everyone seems to know what the group is supposed to be doing, they often have different ideas about what that means. Even if people are saying the same words, those words may mean different things to different people. For example, I remember a group that was established to develop a strategic plan for a division of a large organization. Each member knew what the goal was, but there were different opinions about what developing a strategic plan actually meant. For some, developing a strategic plan meant engaging in a lengthy process of data collection from organization members, competitors, customers; reading literature about their industry; and making predictions of future trends in that industry. Once that information was collected and analyzed, a decision-making process that involved members and customers would be devised. Finally, after this lengthy process, a strategic plan would be enacted.

Others in the group had a very different view of what it meant to develop a strategic plan. For them it meant holding two or three committee meetings, discussing ideas about what the division should do over the next 5 years, and writing up the ideas that the majority of committee members agreed with.

This example underscores the necessity of thorough discussion of group goals and what those goals mean to different group members. Until everyone is clear about those goals, it makes no sense to try to work to accomplish them.

Even after everyone is clear about the group's goal, it does not necessarily follow that everyone agrees with that goal. One of the characteristics of high performance teams, however, is that *members agree with team goals.* That means that people think the goal is reasonable and attainable. Also, people should feel that the goal is important to work on and will benefit the team and the organization.

I do not mean to imply that people must think that the group's goal is the best thing since sliced bread or the most exciting assignment they have ever been given. Some goals (cutting the budget, reducing overhead, changing the shipping schedule) are not very exciting but may be important to the team and the organization. The point is that members need to see the relevance of the goal if the team is to be successful.

— 2. Roles

Once goal clarity and member agreement with the goals has been achieved, group members can begin to organize themselves to accomplish those goals. That usually includes deciding what needs to be done and who should do what in order to achieve those goals.

Using the previous example as a case in point, let's imagine that group members agreed that the tasks involved in developing a strategic plan were as follows:

- Data collection from organization members
- Data collection from competitors
- Data collection from customers
- Reading literature about the current state of their industry
- Reading literature about future trends in their industry
- Analyzing the data
- Developing a decision-making process that involved organization members and customers

After lengthy discussions about how each of these tasks might be accomplished, decisions about what member or members should work on each task need to be made. Often, people volunteer to take on certain tasks or the group leader assigns them to tasks. Neither of these options is inherently good or bad. Three things are crucial, however. First, *each member must be clear about the role he or she is being asked to play*. That is, the expectations are clear, and the process for accomplishing that task is clear as well. Second, *the member must have the ability and skills necessary to accomplish the assigned or chosen task*. Third, *each member must agree with and accept that role assignment*.

Again, these requirements for assigning roles seem obvious. In reality, however, it is the rare group that meets these requirements. The reasons for this failure to ensure that members are clear about their roles, have the abilities necessary to accomplish them, and are willing to take on that role are many. Here are just a few examples of how good people set themselves up to fail:

- Mary volunteers to collect data from organization members. She is new to the company and doesn't know too many people yet. She has worked for three other competitors and would be more valuable in helping to collect information about competitors. Since she volunteered, however, no one is willing to raise any of these issues.
- Joe volunteers to review the literature regarding current and future trends in the industry. He is not computer literate, however, and much of the information will have to be gathered through on-line databases and the Internet. Again, since he volunteered, no one raise these concerns.
- The group's leader, John, volunteers to analyze the data as it comes in. Sarah is a statistician and would be perfect for this job. However, because John is the leader, no one questions his right to assign himself this task.

This group of good and very nice people is engaged in an apparently innocent process that they may live to regret. If changes in the assignments are not made, the chances of group success are extremely remote.

— **3. Interdependence**

In successful teams, *tasks require team members to work together* as a unit and in subgroups. In our previous example, members need to work together as a unit and in subgroups since the amount of work involved in developing a strategic plan is well beyond the scope of a single individual. In addition, the goal of the group requires interdependence because a strategic plan developed by one person is not likely to reflect the division accurately. Finally, a successful strategic plan is one that works. That is, it incorporates many viewpoints, accurately interprets and sifts through those differing views, and develops a plan that will be accepted by others and will lead the division in a positive direction. This is one of the best reasons for using a group versus an individual to accomplish a goal. A well-functioning team will beat an individual in accomplishing this type of goal any day.

— 4. Leadership

In productive teams, the *leader's style changes when necessary to meet emerging group needs*. Member perceptions of the role of the leader change at different stages of group development. In Stage 1, the group perceives the leader as benevolent and powerful. He or she is perceived as the source of member safety and reward. At Stage 1, members expect the leader to be directive. At Stage 2, however, members begin to challenge the leader's authority and control. In order for the group to mature, such challenges are necessary. The role of the leader must be redefined if the group is to move into the more mature stages of development. Stage 2 leaders should still remain directive and gradually begin to involve members in discussing options and exploring issues. By the time a group has reached the third stage of development, group members have assumed many of the roles that initially were the domain of the leader. Finally, at Stage 4, effective leaders act like expert members. Most leader functions have been distributed among team members.

In high performance teams, members assume many of the functions that leaders performed at earlier stages. For this to occur, the leader's role must become less directive and more consultative. Leaders can help to redistribute power among members by altering their leadership style to match the needs of the group. This requires knowing what the needs of the group are at any given time and how to behave in order to facilitate movement. Maintaining one style of leadership throughout the life of a group will not meet group needs and will not facilitate the development of a high performance team. More information about effective leadership can be found in Chapter 6.

— 5. Communication and Feedback

High performance teams have an *open communication structure* that allows all members to participate. Individuals are listened to regardless of their age, title, sex, race, ethnicity, profession, or other status characteristics. This enhances productivity since all ideas and suggestions get heard.

High performance teams also get *regular feedback about their effectiveness and productivity.* When members are asked to assess the team's effectiveness and productivity, they are able to answer accurately. This means that members seek feedback from each other and from external sources about how the team is performing.

Members of high performance teams give each other *constructive feedback about individual performance and contributions.* Constructive feedback promotes improvement and individual development. That is, the feedback is intended to be helpful to the team by improving member efforts to accomplish goals. It also is intended to be helpful to the individual by providing information that he or she can use to become a more effective team member. If feedback does not meet both of these criteria, it should not be given.

Finally, a *high performance team utilizes feedback about team processes and productivity to make improvements in how it is functioning.* You would be surprised at the number of groups that I have encountered whose members receive feedback about group performance but do not use that feedback to implement constructive changes. In most cases, this is due to a simple flaw in the group's internal processes. Groups that do not utilize feedback constructively usually do not have a mechanism in place to evaluate the validity of the feedback and to make decisions about what changes they should make based on that feedback. An example of such a mechanism might be that internal and external feedback is sought on a regular basis and that the feedback is discussed and evaluated at the beginning of the next meeting. If the feedback is judged to be valid and helpful, members discuss ways to improve team performance, decide what changes to make, and implement those changes.

This may seem like an elaborate process, but in reality it usually takes 10 minutes or less. The trick is to collect the feedback from internal members at the end of one session and discuss it at the beginning of the next. Feedback from external sources should be collected between meetings.

— 6. Discussion, Decision Making, and Planning

Members of high performance teams *spend time planning how they will solve problems and make decisions.* That is, they determine how decisions will be made before they attempt to make decisions. They may decide that majority vote, a two-thirds majority vote, consensus, or another decision-making strategy will be employed. The key is that these determinations are made in advance and that *the decision-making strategy is effective* and meets with member approval.

Also, *members of high performance teams spend time defining and discussing problems they must solve.* That is, in advance of a final decision, sufficient discussion has occurred so that everyone is clear about the issues involved and clear about alternative ways of dealing with those issues. If insufficient time is spent in discussion before a decision is made, the resulting decision may be inadequate or in error.

— 7. Implementation and Evaluation

High performance teams *implement the solutions and decisions made by members.* That is, members and the leader follow up on those decisions and hold each other accountable for acting on those decisions. Teams that are successful also develop methods to evaluate team solutions and decisions. Decisions may turn out to be in error or inadequate, but, in effective teams, those errors or inadequacies are caught and corrected quickly.

— 8. Norms and Individual Differences

Successful teams *establish norms that encourage high performance, quality, and success.* Such teams also have *norms that encourage members to be creative and innovative.* It would be difficult, if not impossible, to be successful if members were not expected to perform at high levels.

Another interesting characteristic of effective teams is that *members who behave differently are accepted as long as their behavior is perceived as helpful to task accomplishment.* For example, if a member does not talk as much as other members expect, that member will be accepted as long as the contributions he or she does make are considered helpful. A member who seems loud or a bit aggressive also will be accepted if his or her task-related performance is perceived as useful. In short, successful teams contain members who tolerate, or even enjoy, each other's idiosyncrasies in order to get the job done.

How Do High Performance Teams Function?   45

— 9. Structure

First, successful teams contain *the smallest number of members necessary* to accomplish goals and tasks and no more. Second, the hallmark of a mature team is that members are *able to form subgroups* in order to get work done. Third, those subgroups are not perceived as threatening by other members. Instead, *subgroups are accepted and valued for their contribution to the team.* Subgroups are not seen as renegades or revolutionaries. Rather, subgroups are integrated into the team-as-a-whole. In short, productive teams are organized. They also have *sufficient time together,* overall and at each meeting, to develop and maintain high performance and to accomplish goals.

This last point is worth emphasizing. Having enough time to accomplish goals means that most groups need at least 8 or 9 months together in order to be successful. I base this on the research described earlier that suggests that it takes at least 6 months for groups to mature fully. With regard to the length of individual meetings, that will vary with the complexity of the group's goals. Many meetings simply are too short, however. The most tragic examples of this come, unfortunately, from my work with schools. Elementary, middle, and high school teachers are expected to deal with fairly complicated things. Examples include coordinating the curriculum, developing interdisciplinary lesson plans, and monitoring the behavior and progress of students taught by a number of faculty, just to name a few. In general, the faculty of a school meets as a whole group once a month or less for about an hour or so. Faculty subgroups (e.g., the seventh-grade teachers) meet more frequently. These subgroups usually meet for 45 minutes once a week. Of course, 45 minutes is actually 30 or 35 minutes since teachers need time to dismiss their students and to settle into the meeting. They also have to leave before the end of the allotted time in order to get to their next class on time, making it difficult to have meaningful and thorough discussion, planning, and decision making.

Each group will have to judge for itself how much time will be needed to accomplish its goals and what the length of each meeting should be as well. Don't shortchange the group or set the group up for failure by not allowing enough time. Also, don't use time inefficiently. Individual members and subgroups can do many tasks between meetings.

— 10. Cooperation and Conflict Management

A large body of research confirms that *a high performance team is highly cohesive and contains cooperative members.* Of course, cooperation alone is insufficient to achieve success. The other factors outlined in this chapter must be in evidence as well. For example, in some groups, members cooperate to avoid work. In others, members cooperate to do the minimum amount of work. Clearly, cooperation is not enough, but without it success is very unlikely.

Cooperation does not mean that conflict never occurs. In fact, research tells us that productive teams have frequent, but brief, periods of conflict. Conflicts are brief because high performance teams have effective conflict management strategies.

Productive teams operate differently than unproductive groups. Productivity is not an accident or the result of one or two people. The way a group functions, from the beginning, does make a difference. For example, some recent studies have found that high performance teams actually produce more than other work groups. They also are rated as more productive by their managers, and members rate their teams as more productive. These studies were conducted in the financial industry, the hotel industry, the manufacturing sector, the service sector, and educational institutions.

It's not a waste of time to pay attention to how your group is functioning. Based on what we now know, it's clear that time spent on increasing the functioning of your group is time well spent. It might be helpful for your group to review the characteristics of high performance teams and determine what your group is doing well and what needs improvement. Use the High Performance Team Checklist at the end of this chapter to assess your current level of effectiveness. Collate individual member responses to questions and determine the group's average score. If you score in the nineties, you can legitimately call yourselves members of a high performance team. Regardless of the score, however, there will be areas that need improvement. Plan ways to make necessary improvements.

The High Performance Team Checklist

Organization Name _____

Business/Division, Area Name _____

Group ID Number _____

Member ID Number_____

Date _____

Group Size _____

Please read the statements below. Circle the number that most accurately describes your response to the statement. Use the following key to respond to each statement.

> **1. disagree strongly**
> **2. disagree to some extent**
> **3. agree to some extent**
> **4. agree strongly**

1. Members are clear about group goals.

   1   2   3   4

2. Members agree with group goals.

   1   2   3   4

3. Group tasks require us to work together.

   1   2   3   4

4. Members are clear about their roles.

   1   2   3   4

5. Members accept their roles.

   1   2   3   4

6. Member assignments match their abilities.

   1   2   3   4

7. The group leader's style changes when necessary to meet emerging group needs.

   1   2   3   4

8. We have an open communication structure that allows all members to participate.

   1   2   3   4

9. The group gets regular feedback about its productivity.

1   2   3   4

10. Members give each other constructive feedback.

1   2   3   4

11. The group utilizes feedback about its effectiveness to make improvements in how it is functioning.

1   2   3   4

12. The group spends time defining and discussing problems it must solve.

1   2   3   4

13. Members also spend time planning how they will solve problems and make decisions.

1   2   3   4

14. The group uses effective decision-making strategies.

1   2   3   4

15. The group implements its solutions and decisions.

1   2   3   4

16. The group develops methods to evaluate its solutions and decisions.

1   2   3   4

17. The group accepts members who behave differently as long as their behavior is perceived as helpful to task accomplishment.

1   2   3   4

18. Group norms encourage high performance, quality, and success.

1   2   3   4

19. Group norms encourage innovative solutions.

1   2   3   4

20. Subgroups are accepted and integrated into the group-as-a-whole.

1   2   3   4

21. The group contains the smallest number of members necessary to accomplish its goals.

1   2   3   4

22. The group has been given sufficient time to develop a mature working unit and to accomplish its goals.

1   2   3   4

23. The group is highly cohesive and cooperative.

1   2   3   4

24. Periods of conflict are frequent but brief.

1   2   3   4

25. The group uses effective conflict management strategies.

1   2   3   4

Minimum Score: 25

Maximum Score: 100

My Score:_____

CHAPTER **5**

Effective Team Members

This chapter outlines what we know from research about the behaviors and attitudes of effective team members. These are presented in the form of guidelines. None of these characteristics require any special personality type, but they all require goodwill and some degree of effort. As you read through the chapter, think about a group that you are working with at the moment. Ask yourself the following questions:

- Do I follow these guidelines?
- Can I think of times when I exhibited these behaviors and attitudes?
- Can I think of times when I should have exhibited these behaviors but, for some reason, did not?
- In what areas do I need to improve?
- What do I plan to do in order to improve in those areas?

If you're going to be an effective team member, you'll need to take a close look at your own behaviors and attitudes and at the way you interact with the group. Here are some guidelines to help you evaluate your performance as a group member.

51

Don't Blame Others for Group Problems

One of the more difficult issues I encounter in working with groups is a general feeling of helplessness that individuals frequently express. Somehow, members of groups are convinced that they can't make a difference when it comes to group success. I hear lots of statements like the following:

> "Unless the leader is replaced, there's nothing the rest of us can do."
> "These people are crazy. I don't even want to come to meetings."
> "Team meetings are like swimming with sharks. I just keep my head down."
> "Our meetings are a waste of time. I wish the leader were stronger."
> "I'm not even sure what we're supposed to be doing but I'm afraid to ask."
> "The same people talk in circles. I just keep quiet and hope the meeting will end soon."
> "There's nothing we can do. Upper management has to get into the act before things will change."

I encounter these feelings of helplessness very often among people in the workplace. Of course, I realize that things have been pretty chaotic in organizations due to downsizing, mergers, new initiatives, and the like, but I am not convinced that those are the only reasons for the passivity that I observe. One reason is the human tendency to blame the other guy.

It will probably surprise many readers to learn that there's a social science term that describes this tendency to blame the other guy. It's called the *fundamental attribution error*. What it means is that humans have a tendency to attribute the actions of others to personality characteristics without taking other factors into account. Most of the time that's an error.

Our tendency to blame the boss for poor group results without taking budgetary constraints, the lack of group member cooperation, or the lack of other necessary resources into account is an example of an attribution error. When we say that lack of upper management support is the reason for group failure, despite the fact that many group members don't even come to meetings and no one can agree when they do come, that's an attribution error. When members say that Harry is at fault because he just won't shut up despite the fact that no one else seems willing to talk, that's an attribution error.

Researchers also have uncovered some general patterns about how individual group members interpret group success or failure. For example, leaders and powerful members tend to feel personally responsible for both group success and group failure. Members, on the other hand, take responsibility for team success but not for group failure. Instead, members attribute group failure to leaders, powerful members, the organization, upper management, or other situational constraints.

People tend to misinterpret the behavior and motivations of others. This tendency to misinterpret increases in conflict situations. So, when things aren't going well for the group, we are much more likely to blame others for the situation. While the tendency to misjudge people, events, and actions is natural, it also has very negative effects on the group and on individuals who are wrongly judged.

For example, I often am called upon to assist work groups that are mired in conflict and, as a result, are not within budget or time constraints or are not meeting target goals. There is usually a stable behavior pattern of attacks and counterattacks that has been going on for some time. My goal in working with such a group is to help the group free itself from this pattern and get back on track.

The problem confronting me in such a situation is that because the group is stuck in a pattern of conflict, members tend to be focused on blaming outside forces, other members, or the leader for the group's predicament. As long as blaming is the primary pattern, the group will remain stuck. Also, the longer the blaming continues, the more powerless and frustrated group members will feel.

Changing a pattern of blame to one of collaboration and shared responsibility for group functioning and productivity, however, is no easy task. Schein, a well-known organizational consultant, wrote that the concept of teamwork is inconsistent with the U.S. emphasis on individualism and personal responsibility. Consequently, if the members accept shared responsibility for group functioning, each member will feel compelled to accept personal blame for group failure as well. Resistance to any information that disconfirms the belief that the group's problems are due to the actions of individual members, the leader, or authority figures external to the group is the inevitable result. Unless group members begin to see the situation differently, no change will occur.

One of the most powerful ways that I have found to help members change their view of the situation is to talk with them about the normal, human tendency to blame the other guy. Once members realize that they have made a mistake, they begin to look for other factors that are inhibiting progress. From that point on, changes happen fairly rapidly. Simply put, blaming is a symptom of a negative group pattern. Blaming is almost never a statement of fact. It is rare that one person is responsible for a group's problems. I believe that it is best to assume that is never the case, because that stops the blaming, which often leads the group in a positive direction.

Since I've heard it so many times before, I can almost hear some readers saying that, in their case, the leader really was to blame. Others are thinking it really was that member Harry's fault. Still others are thinking that upper management really was to blame.

I hear these statements so often that it seems as if every leader, on every continent, is incompetent. I hear these statements so frequently that it seems as if every group, on every continent, contains an incompetent, evil, or mentally unbalanced member. This is simply not the case. Most groups contain people who are trying to do a good job. They may not know how. They may not be socially skilled, but they are trying.

My advice is to give everyone the benefit of the doubt not just for his or her sake but for your own and the group's. Blaming does not help. It only starts cycles of revenge and retaliation. Instead, find other factors that might be blocking group progress and fix them. Use some of the checklists in this book to help you determine other things to focus on. You'll be surprised at what happens when you do that. Things start to get better.

By the way, I want to encourage people in management roles to start taking this advice as well. Stop replacing leaders or group members for alleged incompetence. Give teams the resources and training that they need to work together effectively. Supply consultants, if that's necessary. All of us can make attribution errors, and the human cost for these errors is very high.

I started this chapter by introducing the reader to this human tendency to blame the other guy for two reasons. First, it pains me to have repeatedly witnessed these misjudgments and their aftermath (e.g., transfers, firings, hurt feelings, and stress). Second, it was a pretty direct way of saying that all group members and leaders have responsibility for group success and group failings. The rest of the organization does, as well. Chapter 2 outlined what we know from research about what organizations can do to help the groups functioning within them. Chapter 6 will outline what leaders can do to help their groups be successful. This chapter outlines what members can do to help their group be successful. Everybody shares in the responsibility, and that's the truth.

Encourage the Process of Goal, Role, and Task Clarification

Encouraging the process of goal, role, and task clarification is simple to implement. All it means is that when you don't understand what is going on, ask questions until you do. It helps to ask questions of the group and not just the leader, because the discussion that follows will be richer and more likely to really clarify things for everyone.

While this is a very simple thing to do, in the early stages of group development, people hesitate to ask questions. This reticence is quite natural, but try to overcome it a little. Even if you only ask one question of the group, it will make a difference.

Many people have told me that they are afraid to ask questions for fear of being perceived as incompetent or naive. I am quite aware that image is seen as an important thing at work. Despite the old commercial, however, image is not everything. Even if image is very important, asking clarifying questions is unlikely to hurt your image. In fact, it may improve it. Others are most likely to see you as helpful, courageous, or down to earth for asking clarifying questions. None of those qualities is bad for one's image.

Encourage the Adoption of an Open Communication Structure Where All Member Input and Feedback Is Heard

It won't come as a surprise to most readers that some people talk more than others during meetings. Of course, some people are just shy or have less need to be heard than others do. Many, however, talk less because they do not feel invited to speak. This has happened to most of us at one time or another. You go to the first meeting of a group and few people talk to you. When you do say something, very few people respond to what you have said. Think about the kind of group that was and the kind of people it contained. Was there anything about you that was different from the others? Were you

- one of the oldest in the group?
- one of the youngest in the group?
- new to the organization or group?
- one of only a few women in an otherwise male group?
- one of only a few men in an otherwise female group?
- the only one from your profession or area?
- one of only a few minorities in the group?

Were there any other obvious differences between you and other group members?

People tend unconsciously to classify others and assign high or low status to them based on external characteristics, especially during early meetings. Sometimes, it can be things as seemingly meaningless as height, clothes, mannerisms, and the like that get you classified into a high- or low-status position in a group.

By the way, people aren't bad when they classify others and assign them high or low status based on that classification. We all do it, all the time, sometimes without even being aware of what we are doing. In some cases, our tendency to do this can be very helpful. It can keep us out of harm's way. In work groups, however, our tendency to do this can be quite detrimental.

In the beginning of a group, communication patterns get established very quickly. Who talks to whom and who gets to talk a lot or a little becomes clear within a few meetings. No one talks about this. It just happens. The problem with this is that who talks to whom and who gets to talk a lot or a little is usually determined by status characteristics such as age, gender, ethnicity, organizational position, and the like. Once assigned a position in the food chain, it's hard to break out of it.

Women and minorities, for example, tend to be assigned lower status in groups. As a result, they are expected to talk less, and they may be assigned less influential group roles. They often report dissatisfaction with their lower status, and other group members sometimes report uncertainty about the status of minority and female group members.

Group performance suffers when member role and status assignments are inappropriate or when member contributions are ignored. Potentially valuable contributions are overlooked, and goal achievement and productivity suffer as a result. Researchers have identified individual strategies and group conditions, however, that increase the status of women and minorities in groups. These strategies may also be helpful to any individual whose group role or status is not commensurate with his or her abilities.

Individuals who do not accept the lower status assigned to them increase the likelihood of improving their position in the group. People who act in group-oriented, as opposed to individually oriented, ways tend to improve their group status as well. Also, people who demonstrate their competence and abilities to the group tend to increase their status, especially if they have enough time to demonstrate that competence. Eventually, other group members see these demonstrated abilities and there is no longer a need for the individual to prove his or her worth to the group.

Although research has focused mainly on women and minorities, the same advice works for anyone who is perceived as lower in status for whatever reasons. On the individual level, the research suggests that the following strategies can help to elevate one's status in the group:

- Diplomatically resisting an inappropriate role assignment or status
- Demonstrating one's competence and abilities
- Acting in a cooperative, group-oriented way

On the group level, time aids the process of redefinition or reassignment of roles and changes in communication patterns. There's also another factor that helps tremendously. When all members take responsibility to ensure that everyone is heard from and that everyone is clear about and comfortable with their roles, the chances of group success are heightened. Valuable input and skills will be utilized instead of lost.

Ensuring that everyone has the opportunity to be heard can be as simple as stopping periodically to check in with everyone. It takes only a few minutes but can make a big difference in relation to group success.

Promote an Appropriate Ratio of Task and Supportive Communications

In Chapter 3, the importance of supportive comments to group success was discussed. Needless to say, statements focused on the group's work task are very important as well. If we engage only in supportive conversation, we may feel better but won't get much work done. Members of work teams that are successful spend between 60% and 70% of the time talking about goals and tasks. That means that out of 100 statements made by team members, 60 or 70 will be work oriented. The next most frequent kind of statement made in high performance teams will be supportive. The remainder will be statements that express disagreement, focus on topics unrelated to the task, or express some form of dependency. If the proportion of these various kinds of statements changes very much, the group will be less successful.

What this means in practical terms is that when the group strays into an extended conversation about the football game last night, it would be helpful to try to refocus members on the task at hand. Likewise, if the group has been intensely discussing work tasks for an extended period of time, it might be helpful to compliment the group for its efforts or, in some other way, express support. Balance in group conversation, as in life, helps a lot.

Promote the Use of Effective Problem-Solving and Decision-Making Procedures

Effective methods for decision making and problem solving have been studied by a number of researchers. Their results are, in general, overlapping. For example, Shaw stated that effective group problem solving and decision making consists of four steps:

- Recognizing the problem
- Diagnosing the problem
- Making the decision
- Accepting and implementing the decision

Others have outlined a process, similar to Shaw's, that includes the following:

- An orientation phase
- A discussion phase
- A decision phase
- An implementation phase

Each of these phases has significant impact on the quality of a group's solutions and its overall productivity. For example, during the orientation phase the problem is defined and strategies are outlined for solving the problem. Strategies include such things as how to gain needed information about the problem, how to analyze the information, and how to make the final decision. Research tells us that groups that outline these strategies in advance are more successful than are those that do not. Unfortunately, many groups spend little or no time planning strategies for problem solving and decision making. Some groups consider it a waste of time, even if members have been made aware of the fact that planning increases solution quality and group performance.

The amount of time spent in the discussion phase of the problem and potential solutions increases the quality of the outcome. The amount of member participation in the discussion relates to the quality of the group's solution and overall effectiveness as well. Again, many groups do not spend adequate time discussing an issue. In some cases, a group will discuss only a few alternative solutions.

Groups can make the actual decision in a number of ways. The group may delegate the responsibility for the final decision to an individual, a subgroup, or an expert. Member inputs can be averaged to form the basis for decision. Group members can vote on alternative proposals or may choose consensus as their decision-making method. Consensus refers to reaching a decision that is agreeable to all members. Efforts to determine which of these methods is best have been unsuccessful. Individuals like the consensus method, but it does not necessarily produce better decisions. In general, people tend to like any method as long as they can live with the final decision. It is certain, however, that participation in the decision-making process does increase member satisfaction. It may also increase performance to some extent.

Implementing and evaluating group decisions are key elements in the process. Ideally, evaluation is built into the process, and the results of the evaluation form the basis for the group's next problem-solving process. Many of us have sat on committees and made recommendations that were never implemented. This is often the case when the group making the decision does not have the authority to implement its solution. Nothing is as demoralizing to a group. It is incumbent on the group, then, to interact with other groups that will be involved in implementation throughout its deliberations. This increases the likelihood of successful implementation of group outcomes.

These findings suggest that problem solving and decision making are enhanced when groups outline, in advance, the strategies that they will use to solve problems and make decisions. Lengthy discussion of alternative solutions, ensuring implementation and evaluation, and involving all members in these processes also are associated with quality problem solving and decision making.

Encourage the Establishment of Norms That Support Productivity, Innovation, and Freedom of Expression

You might be surprised at the number of groups I encounter that don't expect to generate the best possible product or result. I hear about what group members feel they can get away with and about why time constraints, policies, and lack of resources will prohibit the group from doing a good job. While some of these constraints are very real, if a group agrees to mediocrity, that is what it will get. When groups agree to do the best possible job and to remove as many obstacles from their way as they can, excellence is the likely result.

Freedom of expression was discussed earlier when I advocated the development of an open communication structure. If members do not feel free to offer their ideas about things, it will be difficult for the group to be successful. In this section, I would like to add a few additional comments about freedom of expression.

There has been a great deal of discussion and activity regarding diversity in the workplace for a number of years. There are many good reasons for this. One that is relevant to this discussion is that diversified groups, those made up of people who are different from each other on any number of characteristics (age, ethnicity, sex, profession, skill, knowledge, etc.), tend to make better decisions. To benefit from diversity, however, everyone must be heard and involved in the discussion.

While the emphasis on diversity is, in my estimation, a good thing, I do sometimes worry that some of the differences that are assumed to exist actually do not. A good example of this is the assumption that men and women communicate differently in work groups. For many years, the research on this question was split right down the middle. Some studies concluded that this was true and others that it was not. Most of the studies, however, were conducted in the laboratory and not with real-world groups. When researchers began to study actual work groups, differences between the sexes seemed to disappear. At this point in time, we can conclude that men and women do not communicate differently in work groups. People, regardless of gender, contribute equivalent amounts of hostile, supportive, off-task, and work statements. Although there is less research on other assumed differences, I think that it's best to treat people as individuals and not to make assumptions based on certain categories.

Go Along With Norms That Promote Group Effectiveness and Productivity

Norms are collective value judgments about how members should behave and what should be done in the group. Norms are necessary if group members are to coordinate their efforts and accomplish their goals. Establishing rules or norms about unimportant things or the wrong things, however, has a chilling effect on groups. If, for example, individuals cannot express dissent, things will not go well.

Sometimes norms get established about unimportant things. For example, I know of groups in which members are expected to eat together every day. In others, members are expected to come to work at least an hour before work actually begins. Norms like these may inhibit individual freedom and cause resentment.

On the other hand, some degree of coordination and conformity is necessary for group success. It is important, then, to go along with norms that promote group effectiveness and productivity. While you might have favored a different way of doing things, if the established norm is likely to work, conformity is advised.

The question that arises at this point is which norms encourage productivity? Research tells us that norms encouraging high performance standards and effectiveness increase team productivity. Shared expectations of success also support productivity. A norm that encourages innovation increases the likelihood of higher productivity as well. Norms and values that support superior quality, service, innovation, and attention to detail significantly increase team effectiveness and productivity. Make sure that your team has norms like these and does not create other norms that block effectiveness, and things will go well.

Promote Group Cohesion and Cooperation

The following are some of the positive effects of cohesion in groups:

- Increased conformity
- Increased group influence over its members
- Increased member satisfaction with the group
- Increased group integration
- Increased cooperation

Cooperation, which is facilitated by cohesion and shared goals, has many positive effects on group functioning. The characteristics of cooperative groups are listed next:

- More effective communication
- Friendlier group atmosphere
- Stronger individual desire to work on group tasks
- Stronger feelings of commitment to the group
- Greater division of labor
- Greater coordination of effort

- Greater productivity
- Increased trust and the development of lasting agreements
- Increased ability to resolve conflicts

A word of caution with regard to cohesion is appropriate at this point. High levels of cohesion, in conjunction with certain other factors, can have negative effects. That is, a group can make poor or, in some cases, danger-ous decisions due to an overriding wish to maintain unity and cohesion. This leads the group to overlook other choices or courses of action. If a group is cohesive and also has the following characteristics, it may be in danger of making poor decisions, a condition that is referred to as "group-think":

- When groups deliberate in relative isolation and do not report, or check, their conclusions with others outside the group, the possi-bility of poor decisions increases.
- If the group's leader controls the discussion and makes his or her po-sitions clear from the outset, poor group decisions are more likely.
- If the group is faced with a major and stressful decision, the tendency to decide quickly in order to reduce the stress is enhanced. This often results in poor decisions as well.

Cohesion alone does not pose a threat. As long as a group stays con-nected with others outside the group and has an effective leader, high lev-els of cohesion will have many positive effects on group productivity. How, then, can group members promote cohesion? Research tells us that when goals and methods to reach those goals are clear, cohesion increases. Also, successful conflict resolution reduces individual fears of rejection and increases trust among members. A feeling of "we-ness," or cohesive-ness, results. Finally, while it is rarely clear what causes what in an inter-acting system, increased communication is associated with increased co-hesion and vice versa.

The reader will notice that the research does not suggest that sharing personal feelings, developing personal friendships, socializing outside of work, or other similar things increase group cohesion. It is not necessary to know other group members on a personal level in order to promote co-

---

BOX 5.1
Group Therapy?

I got a call from a group leader. He said his group was a mess. When I asked what was happening, he gave me a lengthy personality profile of each group member. He also told me how each person related to other members and who was feuding with whom. The group's problem turned out to be due to a lack of clarity about goals and tasks. When these issues were straightened out, the "personality problems" went away. Psychoanalysis was not necessary.

---

hesion. Working to increase goal clarity and communication should occur in the work group. Conflict resolution should as well.

Encourage the Use of Effective Conflict Management Strategies

Conflicts continue to occur throughout a group's life. In fact, group conflict is almost as common as group cooperation. One could conclude that conflict seriously impairs group cohesion. While this can be the result, cohesion can also be positively affected by conflict. Although this sounds paradoxical, it is important to note that, in any relationship, the freedom to be oneself and to disagree without fear of rejection or retribution increases, rather than decreases, cohesion and trust. Also, conflict provides energy to the group and allows for clarification of group values, goals, and structures. All of these have been found to be associated with increased cohesion and trust. Cohesion and conflict are linked. You can't have one without the other, so to speak.

Of course, how conflict is dealt with is the crucial factor in determining its effect on cohesion. Inevitably, conflict is resolved. How it is resolved will determine whether group cohesion is positively or negatively affected. Six methods of conflict resolution have been described by a number of researchers:

- Imposition of the position of an individual or subgroup on other members
- Withdrawal of an individual or subgroup from the group
- Inaction, where one or both sides of a conflict do nothing to resolve the conflict
- Yielding, where one side gives up its position
- Compromise, where the parties find a solution somewhere between their respective positions
- Problem solving, where the source of the conflict is located and a mutually agreeable solution is found

The first four solutions have many negative repercussions. Imposition can result in hostility and passive-aggressive behavior on the part of group members. Withdrawal threatens the life of the group and reduces its resources through member loss. Inaction can result in simmering discontent, apathy, or alienation. Yielding may also elicit alienation and covert hostility. Compromise can be viable if the resolution of the conflict seems reasonable and acceptable to all concerned. Problem solving, however, gives the best results because it requires the actual resolution of different perspectives and a new group conceptualization of the issues involved in the conflict.

Some groups navigate their conflicts well, and others disband or become dysfunctional by dealing with their differences ineffectively. What do successful teams do to promote positive conflict resolution? Members of successful teams communicate their views clearly and explicitly. They avoid generalizations and are specific in their communication. They talk about trust and cooperation during the discussion. Members also initially respond cooperatively to others who are behaving competitively. If others continue to respond competitively, successful group members demonstrate their willingness to compete by arguing their position. While this sounds like an inappropriate strategy, research suggests that this may result in cooperation from others since not to do so would result in continued stress or personal losses. Sometimes, demonstrating a willingness to compete will bring about cooperation from others. Demonstrating a willingness to compete may also result in being viewed as a more formidable opponent.

All of these strategies help maintain a reasonable trust level, which allows negotiations to proceed. Negotiation is an important conflict reso lution strategy. Seeking a mutually agreeable, or win-win, solution has been found to increase communication and cooperation. It also tends to reduce the conflict by breaking it down into specific issues that can be dealt with one at a time.

Sometimes, the intensity and depth of the conflict is too great to be solved by the group members themselves. In such cases, seeking the aid of a third party can help resolve the conflict. Group and organizational consultants are often asked to assist groups that are stuck as a result of seemingly insurmountable conflicts. This can be a useful strategy for conflict resolution. However, third-party intervention should be sought only if all parties want the help and if the intensity of the conflict is high. This last-resort strategy requires willingness on the part of the group and considerable skill on the part of the third party.

Interact With Others Outside the Group in Ways That Promote Group Integration and Cooperation Within the Larger Organizational Context

Ancona, a group researcher, argued that mature, internal group functioning is not enough to ensure group effectiveness. Groups and their members must regularly interact with the rest of the organization in order to be successful. Groups need support from and information about what is going on in the rest of the organization. Ancona proposed four key external activities that group members should perform. These activities are described next.

Negotiation with other groups and individuals external to the group is necessary to secure needed resources. For example, some group members might be designated to serve on interdepartmental committees or to meet with other groups or individuals in an attempt to influence policies concerning such things as organizational distribution of resources or procedural decisions. Negotiation with other groups is also necessary when conflicts arise.

Information exchange and scanning involves gathering facts and impressions from other parts of the organization in order to determine current and future conditions and their potential impact on the group. These

---

BOX 5.2
Interspecies Conflict

An organization dedicated to animal welfare reorganized its employees into species-specific teams. Soon after, the Whale team and the Seal team began to fight over resources. The Whale team was accused of throwing its weight around.

---

activities help the group adapt to the environment and make decisions regarding how to respond to these conditions.

Buffering entails protecting the group from too much external information or pressure. Some members may perform the role of sentry or guard to insulate the group from excessive external demands. Buffering is sometimes necessary since too much input can negatively affect internal group processes. If buffering is used as a strategy for too long, however, it may encourage an isolationist stance that will decrease communication with others and reduce the likelihood of group success as a result.

Strategic management and profile management involve communicating with external individuals and groups in order to influence their perceptions of and behaviors toward your group. How a group is perceived by other groups in the organization affects the group by either increasing or decreasing the willingness of others to provide resources to or to work with that group. Groups can consciously help shape their image by planning what information they will share with others.

Support the Leader's Efforts to Facilitate Group Goal Achievement

This chapter began with a discussion of the fact that many group members blame the leader for group problems and failures. Effective team members, however, do the opposite. That is, they support the leader's efforts to coordinate and facilitate the group. Effective team members volunteer to perform tasks that need to be done. They also ask questions for clarification, offer advice to the leader when appropriate, and in many other ways actively participate in the leadership function. Group development and effectiveness hinge on the willingness of members to assume some leadership functions and the willingness of leaders to delegate those functions.

The Effective Member Checklist summarizes what has been discussed about effective membership. Spend some time and check yourself. How could you improve? Encourage other group members to do likewise.

Effective Member Checklist

Please read the statements below. Circle the number that most accurately describes your response to the statement. Use the following key to respond to each statement.

1. **disagree strongly**
2. **disagree to some extent**
3. **agree to some extent**
4. **agree strongly**

1. I avoid blaming others for group problems.

   1   2   3   4

2. I assume that every group member is trying to do a good job.

   1   2   3   4

3. I encourage the process of goal, role, and task clarification.

   1   2   3   4

4. I work to ensure that the input and feedback of every member is heard.

   1   2   3   4

5. I work to ensure that we all have the chance to demonstrate our competence and skills in the group.

   1   2   3   4

6. I act, and encourage others to act, in the best interests of the group.

   1   2   3   4

7. When members stray off the task, I diplomatically try to bring the discussion back to that task.

   1   2   3   4

8. When members contribute good ideas, I express my appreciation.

    1   2   3   4

9. I encourage the use of effective problem-solving and decision-making procedures.

    1   2   3   4

10. I encourage the group to outline, in advance, the strategies that will be used to solve problems and make decisions.

    1   2   3   4

11. I work to ensure that decisions and solutions are implemented and evaluated.

    1   2   3   4

12. I encourage norms that support productivity, innovation, and freedom of expression.

    1   2   3   4

13. I treat people as individuals and don't make assumptions about them based on my preconceived notions about people like them.

    1   2   3   4

14. I discourage any group tendency to adopt excessive or unnecessary norms.

    1   2   3   4

15. I go along with norms that promote group effectiveness and productivity.

    1   2   3   4

16. I encourage high performance standards.

    1   2   3   4

17. I expect the group to be successful and productive.

    1   2   3   4

18. I encourage innovative ideas.

    1   2   3   4

19. I am, and encourage others to be, cooperative.

    1   2   3   4

20. I encourage the use of effective conflict management strategies.

    1   2   3   4

21. In conflict situations, I communicate my views clearly and explicitly.

1   2   3   4

22. I respond cooperatively to others who are behaving competitively.

1   2   3   4

23. I encourage and work to achieve mutually agreeable solutions to conflict.

1   2   3   4

24. I have negotiated, or would be willing to negotiate, with other groups and individuals to help my group obtain needed resources.

1   2   3   4

25. I share information and impressions I have about other parts of the organization with the group.

1   2   3   4

26. I encourage the group not to overwhelm itself with too much external information or demands.

1   2   3   4

27. I talk positively about my group with outsiders.

1   2   3   4

28. I keep other members of the organization informed about what my group is doing.

1   2   3   4

29. I support division of labor necessary to accomplish group goals.

1   2   3   4

30. I use what I have learned about group development and productivity to help my group become effective.

1   2   3   4

31. I encourage the group to assess and alter its functioning frequently, if necessary.

1   2   3   4

32. I do not get bogged down in interpersonal issues or personality conflicts.

1   2   3   4

33. I support the leader's efforts to coordinate and facilitate group goal achievement.

1   2   3   4

34. I volunteer to perform tasks that need to be done.

1   2   3   4

35. I offer advice to the leader when I think the advice will be helpful.

1   2   3   4

Minimum Score: 35

Maximum Score: 140

My Score: _____

6

CHAPTER

Effective Team Leadership

The belief that leaders are instrumental in the creation of effective teams is deeply rooted in society and in the social sciences. Today's conceptions of leadership are not very different from early views, which described leaders as individuals who possessed special inborn characteristics that propelled them into leadership roles. Now, most social scientists reject the notion of inborn traits. Many still see leadership as residing in the individual, however, because it is assumed that individuals can learn how to be effective leaders by acquiring certain knowledge and skills. Hundreds of thousands of managers and executives have attended leadership training programs over the years in quests to learn to be effective leaders.

Leaders are thought to facilitate the development of shared understandings and interpretations of reality among group members. They articulate things that have not been explicitly stated before that can provide new visions for the group. Inherent in this position is the assumption that the leadership role is vital to the creation and maintenance of an effective team. This assumption has led some researchers to study the cognitive capacities of leaders in order to determine how effective leaders think about their role. Again, such studies have as a goal the discovery of effective leadership styles that could then be taught to other leaders or potential leaders.

Recently, the old notion of the charismatic leader is receiving renewed attention. In this view, the leader is seen as one who instills new thinking in followers and redirects group activities. Such descriptions of leadership continue to support the assumption that leaders are central to the creation and redirection of group culture. In fact, leaders are perceived as having so much power that, should they act in selfish or unethical ways, great damage can be done to the group and its members. Leaders are clearly perceived as capable of making a significant difference in groups.

For the average person in a leadership role in the workplace, these views of leaders as crucial to group success can be overwhelming. It's all up to you. If the group fails, it's your fault. The stress of this enormous personal responsibility can have negative effects on potential or actual leaders. Potential leaders may choose not to become leaders, and actual leaders may suffer emotional or physical stress as a result of this sense of tremendous responsibility.

There are some social scientists who disagree with the prevailing, relatively one-sided view of the leader as central to team effectiveness and success. Some speak to the interdependence of leaders, followers, and the dynamic forces in which a group is operating. In this view, all group members share the responsibility for the creation of an effective team. Multiple discussions among all members eventually result in shared assumptions about goals and the methods to accomplish those goals. Leaders are part of this process but are not necessarily a primary part. Group success or failure is the result of many mutual influences.

Group development theories also suggest that a group's culture and structure are the products of processes inherent in groups. This view of the creation of effective teams is not as leader-centric. The creation of group culture is seen as the result of inherent forces. The content of culture in different groups is not uniform as a consequence. Rather, the particulars of a culture result from the resolution of differences and disagreements that emerge in that group. The process, however, is the same from group to group, and all members are involved in the creation of that group's unique culture and structure.

While minority opinions such as those just reviewed do exist, the majority view of leaders as key to group success dominates our thinking. In this chapter, I reduce that domination a bit and reduce the overwhelming feeling of responsibility associated with leadership in today's work environment. I present guidelines for leaders about what they can do to help their groups become effective and productive teams. As has been the case throughout this book, the guidelines are based on research. Inherent in these guidelines is an assumption of mine, which is that leaders alone cannot be held responsible for group success or failure. Having reviewed the leadership research, I am convinced that the view of groups as interdependent systems is the more accurate one. I have already alluded to this assumption in previous chapters. In fact, two of the preceding chapters could not have been written if I believed that leaders were ultimately responsible for group outcomes. The larger organization, external conditions, and members also influence group success or failure. While leaders can help or hinder the process, so can others.

I also want to dispel the myth that leaders must be special people with a tremendous amount of skill in order to be effective. The average person of goodwill, who is flexible and willing to learn some basic skills, can be an effective leader. Not all situations require leaders of exceptional skill. In fact, in many group situations, charismatic leaders may inhibit group progress because their dominating presence may reduce member participation and motivation to take on certain tasks necessary for group success. Groups work well when all members actively participate. If leaders remain prominent throughout group life, groups will be less likely to succeed. With these assumptions as a foundation, the following guidelines for effective leadership are suggested. As you read through the chapter, think about a group that you are leading at the moment or have recently led. Ask yourself the following questions:

1. Do I follow these guidelines?
2. Can I think of examples of times when I exhibited these behaviors or attitudes?
3. Can I think of times when I should have exhibited these behaviors or attitudes but, for some reason, did not?
4. In what areas do I need to improve?
5. What do I plan to do in order to improve in those areas?

There are certain things you must keep in mind and certain things you must do if you are going to be an effective team leader. The following guidelines outline how leaders become effective.

Don't Take On Every Leadership Assignment You Are Offered

Research attempts to determine the personal characteristics of effective leaders have a long and disappointing history. The search for leadership traits did not result in many consistent findings. Despite all the effort, only a few traits have been consistently identified. Effective leaders tend to have more task-related abilities. They also are more social and more motivated to be leaders than others.

While these findings indicate that a few personal characteristics do influence leadership capabilities, it is important to note that task-related abilities will vary in different situations. The same is true of the kinds of social skills required of leaders in different situations. The same individual will not necessarily be an effective leader in every context as a result.

An effective leader of an engineering product development team, for example, might be ineffective as leader of a group in the financial or hotel industry. Knowledge of the tasks of a group in another industry would, in all likelihood, be lacking. Although this may seem self-evident, in large organizations composed of many different businesses, people are often transferred among businesses without regard to task competence. Such transfers are based on the assumption that effective leaders will be effective in a variety of contexts and that knowledge of a group's task is not essential for leadership. Research suggests that this is not the case. To be effective, leaders must understand the work of a group.

The social skills required in different leadership roles also vary. An outgoing, engaging, and charming style might be required in some situations. In others, a more sedate, low-key style works best. While some people may be able to adjust their styles to meet different social demands, others may not be as successful. All leaders must adjust their styles at different times in order to facilitate group progress. However, certain personality characteristics are difficult to alter, and task competence in very different areas is difficult to come by. The bottom line, then, is that it is best to be selective about the leadership roles you take on. Choose to take on a leadership role when you understand the group's work and you believe that you will be able to meet group needs.

Adjust Your Leadership Style to Meet the Developmental Needs of the Group at a Particular Point in Time

Member perceptions of the role of the leader change at different stages of group development. In Stage 1, the group perceives the leader as benevolent and powerful. He or she is perceived as the source of member safety and reward. In Stage 2, members begin to challenge the leader's authority and control. In order for the group to mature, such challenges are necessary. The role of the leader must be redefined if the group is to move into the more mature stages of development. Power is redistributed, and all group leaders experience some loss of influence and prominence as those groups mature.

Groups that successfully move through the developmental sequence do so, in part, by changing the relationship between members and the leader. The leader—once benevolent, then authoritarian in the eyes of members—emerges in later stages as a more realistic group facilitator and coordinator. Earlier mythic qualities ascribed to the leader by members are stripped away and a human being with a job to do emerges. Leader prominence is less necessary in later stages of development because goals and roles have become clear. Member roles have emerged that take over certain aspects of the leader's role. The elaborated group social structure makes leader prominence unnecessary and potentially disruptive. The leader moves into a more consultative role when groups become teams. Leadership is still necessary for coordination; however, both leaders and members provide that coordination.

These changes in status and perceptions take their toll on the bravest of leaders. Because most people who assume a leadership role are not aware of these naturally occurring group processes, they may feel defeated as a result of attacks and challenges to their authority that occur in

Stage 2. However, for the group to develop further, the leader's role must be significantly altered.

In mature and productive teams, members assume many of the functions that leaders performed at earlier stages. For this to occur, the leader's role must become less directive and more consultative. Leaders can help to redistribute power among members by altering their leadership style to match the needs of the group. This requires knowing what the needs of the group are at any given time and how to behave in order to facilitate movement. Maintaining one style of leadership throughout the life of a group will not meet group needs and will not facilitate the development of an effective and productive team. The question for leaders, then, is, "What leadership style is best at the different stages of group development?" The following guidelines suggest ways for leaders to behave when groups are in the different stages of group development.

Leadership at Stage 1

— Be a Directive and Confident Leader With a Stage 1 Group

In a new group, members expect leaders to be directive, confident, organized, and task oriented. Group members have not had the time to organize themselves yet. That will come later. In the meantime, members want the leader to provide that structure for them. Don't be afraid to do that. Many new leaders feel that it is best to ask members to help structure the group from the very beginning. While this may seem democratic and right, it tends to make members feel insecure and slows group progress.

Come into meetings with a clear, written agenda. State the group's goals as clearly as possible. Run meetings efficiently and assign tasks to individuals as necessary. If decisions are called for, make them. Your initial attempts to organize things will be modified later as group members become more involved. In the beginning, however, providing direction and appearing confident of group success is essential.

— Work to Reduce Member Anxiety, Fears of Rejection, and Concerns About Safety

In the first stage of group development, member dependency, anxiety, and needs for inclusion and safety are at their height. The leader is likely to be seen as benevolent, competent, and the provider of safety to anxious group members. One of the leader's main jobs during this time is to reduce the anxieties of group members. Leaders can reduce member anxiety by expressing confidence and providing direction. In addition, it is important to be fair and sensitive when dealing with members. Make sure that you don't put individuals on the spot or react negatively to anyone. Also, help members to feel included by addressing people by name and inviting members to participate. Initially, inviting participation is helpful. Insisting on participation or singling out nonparticipators, however, is not helpful.

— Provide Positive Feedback

In the beginning of a group, positive feedback from the leader increases cohesion. Using your leadership position to reward rather than punish members, then, will facilitate group development. There are many ways to accomplish this. Thanking people for their attendance, input, and ideas are just some of the ways to provide positive feedback.

— Facilitate Open Discussion of Goals, Values, and Tasks

In the first stage of group development, leaders play an important role in facilitating group growth. This is so because leaders have the most clearly defined role during this period. Since development is progressive, the task of a leader at Stage 1 is to facilitate movement to the next developmental phase. That is, the leader's task is to act in ways that will precipitate open discussion of values, goals, tasks, and leadership so that differences of opinion regarding these elements of group life can surface. This will move the group in the direction of Stage 2. Since people are hesitant to express different opinions at Stage 1, it is sometimes useful to ask people to express their views anonymously. This can be accomplished by asking people to write down their views on a specific issue. Next, those views can be summarized and shared with all members. This makes open discussion of divergent opinions much easier because no individual has to claim responsibility for expressing a difference of opinion or for being the first to disagree with a particular view.

— Facilitate Member Feelings of Competence by Providing Supervision, Training, and Education in Task- and Process-Related Activities

It is important for members to feel competent in relation to group goals and tasks. In some groups, members enter the group with considerable skill. However, skill levels may not be the same for all group members. It is helpful to review the skills necessary to accomplish the group's tasks with all members in order to ensure that everyone is "on the same page."

Training in group participation skills is as important as training in task-related skills. Typically, group leaders have received much more training about groups than members have received. As was stated earlier, hundreds of thousands of people have attended leadership training. I know of very few membership training seminars, except those that I conduct myself. The assumption seems to be that if leaders understand how groups operate, they will be able to make those groups and their members behave effectively. This is not the case. Members are vital to group success and require the same knowledge and skill about group participation that leaders require.

If certain necessary skills in either the task or group participation areas are lacking, training, education, supervision, or a combination of these may be required to ensure group success. Again, members are unlikely to ask for these things at this early stage of development. Therefore, it is incumbent on leaders to determine what member skill levels are and which skills might need strengthening. Anonymous surveys or private interviews with group members may be helpful in this regard.

— Set High Performance Standards and Provide Guidance as Needed

Research tells us that groups with high performance standards tend to be more successful. Setting those standards from the beginning is therefore very important. During discussions of goals, then, it is helpful not only to describe the product that the group is expected to generate but also to discuss expectations regarding the quality of that product. It also is helpful to review standards for group participation. Use the Effective Member Checklist and the Effective Leader Checklist as ways of setting performance standards for member and leader participation.

— Manage the External Environment for the Group

One of the important functions leaders must perform during the early stages of group development is managing the group's interaction with the rest of the organization. Later on, members will take over some aspects of this function. Initially, however, it falls to the leader to negotiate with other groups and individuals for needed resources, buffer the group from excessive external demands, and report on group progress as a way of ensuring that the group is regarded positively by the rest of the organization.

Leadership at Stage 2

— When Members Begin to Demand More Participation in Running the Group, Slowly Begin to Empower Them to Have It

In the first stage of group development, leaders have considerable influence. Members tend to be dependent on the leader for direction and safety. Leaders have a good deal of influence with regard to initial definition of goals and preliminary decisions about the type of group structure being established. The leader is expected by group members to provide direction, safety, order, and group goals and structures. Attempts to engage members in these activities at Stage 1 would be futile.

During Stage 2, however, member expectations and reactions to the leader change quite a bit. As members become more comfortable in the group, they begin to resent what is now perceived as undue influence on the part of the leader. The leader's competence may be challenged. Some members may feel manipulated by the leader. The safety and competence that members perceived the leader as providing is questioned. Suspicion of and challenges to the leader's authority often begin to take place.

Not all members become disenchanted with the leader. Some remain loyal. The group may split into two factions over this issue. One faction is supportive of the leader and the other is not. These two factions often fight about their expectations of the leader and his or her performance with regard to those expectations. Some of this conflict may be due to actual leader behavior in the group. Much of the conflict, however, is about things that go beyond the role of the leader. In essence, the conflict with and about the leader is a way for the group to discuss who can have input into decisions. Roles and decision-making, power, status, and communication structures are being clarified in this process. Efforts to redistribute power begin to occur as well. These are all necessary for group progress.

During the first stage of group development, the role of leader is the most differentiated and important role. Other roles are just being assigned. The leader role is necessary to the establishment of some sense of safety and order. In effect, the role of leader and members' reactions to that role are the impetus for the emergence of other roles and structures in the group. The prominence of the leader at Stage 1 and member dependence on the leader, then, allows for initial structures to form. Once these are in place, the group can begin to define its structure even further. A major way that the group does this is by redefining the leader's role and reducing, to some extent, the power associated with that role. This redistribution of power clears the way for other structures and roles to emerge.

So far, this seems like a reasonable and natural transition. However, leaders have used their power during Stage 1. The acquisition of power tends to make individuals want more power, not less. Thus, the redistribution of power necessary for further group development is not an easy process. When leaders are met with resistance, their efforts to exert power and influence tend to increase, not decrease.

Three types of power have been described in the literature. There is *power over,* which is associated with dominance. *Power from* is the ability to resist unwanted influence and demands. *Power to, or empowerment,* is the ability to act more freely through power sharing. Power-over strategies tend to have negative effects on group relationships and goal achievement. Such leadership tactics often push others to attempt to take power from the leader, and conflict is the inevitable result. Leaders who employ power-to, or empowering, strategies facilitate group development since no leader can perform all the functions of leadership alone. Redistribution of power is essential to facilitate group development and productivity.

Given the previous discussion, a group is not always successful in altering its perceptions, or the leader's perceptions, of the leadership role. Also, even if the group's perceptions change, the leader may force or coerce the group into continuing to respond as it did in Stage 1. Should the group fail to alter its perceptions, it will regress to the dependency stage of group development. Should the leader and group disagree about the leader's role and be unable to resolve this controversy, a prolonged fight for power and control is likely to occur. The group remains in Stage 2 for an extended period of time. Should that happen, the group's cohesion, social structure, and productivity will be very adversely affected. Power struggles, fights, and the like will take precedence over goal achievement, efficiency, and productivity.

Effective leaders expect challenges to their authority and expect member demands for more participation in running the group. These leaders see those challenges and demands as a positive sign of group progress and not as threats to their authority. They respond to these challenges by slowly beginning to empower group members to participate more equally in group management functions. Effective leaders do this slowly since it will take members some time to work out conflicts and roles with regard to group management. Giving up the reins all at once could be disruptive. A slower redistribution of power will be most effective.

— Don't Take Attacks and Challenges Personally

One of the reasons why groups fail to resolve the tension and conflict inherent in this stage of group development is that leaders and members tend to personalize the experience. That is, when others challenge an individual member's views, the individual has a natural tendency to feel hurt and personally attacked. Leaders who are attacked or discounted by members also tend to perceive these as personal affronts. As a result, individuals may become quite defensive and combative. This escalation of tension to unmanageable levels may significantly reduce the group's chances of resolving conflict and creating a unified group culture and structure.

BOX 6.1
Revenge and Retaliation

This college had four deans in as many years. I thought of the faculty as the "dean slayers." The new dean wanted me to help him create a good working relationship with the faculty. For a while, things went pretty well. The faculty had challenged his authority and questioned his competence, but he did not take the bait. Finally, a faculty member wrote to the president of the University complaining about the dean. The dean retaliated and full-scale war broke out. He is no longer dean.

Adopting a group perspective can be very helpful to members and leaders, especially at this stage. If the events of Stage 2 are viewed from this perspective, they are understood very differently. Rather than feel personally attacked, a leader, with a group perspective, could view the attack as a sign that the group is ready to define its structure further. The leader would view his role at this stage as a focus or catalyst for continued development. He or she would not feel threatened by the loss of some power or influence. Rather, the leader might come to view this redistribution of power roles and tasks as essential to group productivity and goal achievement.

In like fashion, a member whose views are challenged by others could see the challenges as necessary to the establishment of shared goals and an integrated group culture and social structure. Instead of reacting defensively, the member might focus on clarifying his or her views and the views of others in an attempt to gain consensus. A group perspective makes it possible for individuals to view conflict as normal and necessary at this stage of group development.

In real situations, I have seen the positive effects of adopting a group perspective on numerous occasions. If a group that is stuck in the conflict stage can adopt a group perspective, it may be able to free itself and move to higher developmental stages. The first step, then, is learning about group development and dynamics. Simply knowing about these phenomena, however, is not enough. Leaders and members must be able to give up blaming each other in order to begin to resolve the conflicts. This is not easy. Even though we know intellectually that conflict, attacks, and disagreements are normal and necessary parts of group development, on an emotional level we may feel hurt or angry. Our emotions may overwhelm us and lead us to seek revenge or vindication rather than reconciliation and consensus. In many cases, group members and leaders would rather "get even" than succeed.

— Act in Ways That Facilitate Open Discussion and Resolution of Conflicts Regarding Values, Goals, and Leadership

Conflict resolution increases group cohesion and trust, which makes it possible for the group to focus on strategies to achieve shared goals. In short, it moves the group in the direction of the third stage of group development. Some strategies to manage conflict were discussed in the previous chapter. They are briefly outlined again here because both members and leaders have responsibility for discussion and resolution of conflicts.

Leaders and members of successful teams communicate their views clearly and explicitly. They avoid generalizations and are specific in their communication. They talk about trust and cooperation during the discussion. Leaders and members also initially respond cooperatively to others who are behaving competitively. If others continue to respond competitively, successful group leaders and members demonstrate their willingness to compete by arguing their position.

Negotiation is an important conflict resolution strategy. Seeking a mutually agreeable solution has been found to increase communication and cooperation. It also tends to reduce the conflict by breaking it down into specific issues that can be dealt with one at a time.

When the intensity and depth of the conflict is too great to be solved by the group members themselves, seeking the aid of a third party can help resolve the conflict. Third-party intervention should be sought only if all parties want the help and if the intensity of the conflict is high. This last-resort strategy requires willingness on the part of the group and considerable skill on the part of the third party.

Leadership at Stage 3

— Involve Members in the Leadership
Function of the Group

Involving members as participants in the leadership process is the hallmark of Stage 3 leadership. Since leaders cannot perform every task, delegation and power sharing are necessary and indicative of an effective leadership style.

Leader prominence is less necessary at later stages of development because goals and roles have become clear. Member roles have emerged that take over aspects of the leader's role. The elaborated group structure makes leader prominence unnecessary and potentially disruptive. The leader moves into a more consultative role with the group. Leadership is still necessary for coordination; however, that coordination function now is shared among members and the leader. The following guidelines describe what effective leaders do at Stage 3.

— Encourage and Support Member Efforts to
Share in the Leadership Function of the Group

In Stage 3, members are ready to facilitate meetings or portions of meetings. By this time, they are capable of working in subgroups to accomplish goals. Members will be giving reports about subgroup meetings and about tasks that have been accomplished between meetings. They will be involved in decision making and conflict resolution. Members also will be involved in negotiation, scanning, buffering, and group image and profile management within the larger organization. In short, members will have assumed many of the functions performed solely by the leader at earlier stages of development.

The leader is freed up to act more as a consultant to and supporter of members. The tasks of both leaders and members of Stage 3 groups are the same. By this time, the power differential between leaders and followers has been reduced and participants are operating in more egalitarian ways. All participants share equal responsibility for and commitment to the group. Their shared task is to consolidate gains in trust and cohesion and to organize themselves in ways that will ensure group productivity. Leaders who support, compliment, and praise member efforts to share in the leadership function will increase the likelihood of group success.

— Encourage the Group to Make Any Necessary Changes in the Group's Structure That Will Facilitate Group Productivity

One of the primary tasks of a Stage 3 group is to assess how it is functioning and to make any adjustments that will facilitate group productivity. Leaders encourage members to do this but do not do the work for the group. Instead, they provide ways for members to identify issues that may impede productivity and to determine ways to remove those impediments. They also participate, along with members, in identifying impediments to group success and in planning strategies to overcome those impediments. The checklists in previous chapters could be used as one way to approach this task.

Leadership at Stage 4

— Participate as an Expert Member of Your Team

Leaders of Stage 4 teams can relax a little bit. Things should be going pretty smoothly. Members have taken on responsibilities and are actively pursuing group goal achievement. Leaders continue to act as consultants, as needed. In general, however, they participate along with members in achieving objectives and team success.

— Continue to Monitor Team Processes, Especially for Signs of Regression

Each time a member leaves, new tasks are added, external conditions change, or other factors shift in some significant way, team dynamics are affected. In each of these circumstances, the team will experience disruptions, and adjustments will be required to regain former levels of cohesion and productivity. Awareness and discussion of this fact of team life on the part of leaders and members is essential. Leaders and members can help maintain team effectiveness by periodically assessing the team and identifying issues that need to be addressed. In this way, a team can continually monitor its functioning and make necessary adjustments. Ways to conduct these periodic assessments are described in Chapter 10.

No team or individual sustains high levels of productivity for long periods of time. People and groups require periods of rest, relaxation, flight, "grumpiness," and fun. Unrealistic expectations of our human capacities may be one of the biggest threats to individual and team effectiveness.

— Conduct Organizational Support Reviews Regularly

In Chapter 2, the importance of organizational support to team success was discussed. I recommended that relevant external individuals and groups meet with the team on a regular basis to assess the adequacy of that organizational support and to plan ways to increase the level of support, if necessary. I want to encourage leaders to ensure that these reviews happen regularly throughout the life of the group. The frequency of reviews will vary from group to group, depending on the time frame allotted to the group to accomplish its work. For example, if a product development group has 18 months to accomplish its goal, I would suggest a review at the very beginning, one about 3 months later, and then at longer intervals. Do what makes sense for your group.

— Regardless of the Stage Your Group Is In, Be an Effective Group Member

Leaders also must be effective group members. Review the Effective Member Checklist in Chapter 5 to assess how well you are doing in that regard. Also, review the Effective Leader Checklist provided next to assess how well you are doing in your current leadership role.

Effective Leader Checklist

Please read the statements below. Circle the number that most accurately describes your response to the statement. Use the following key to respond to each statement.

1. disagree strongly
2. disagree to some extent
3. agree to some extent
4. agree strongly

1. I avoid taking leadership assignments for which I do not have sufficient task-related knowledge.

    1   2   3   4

2. I avoid taking leadership assignments for which I do not have the appropriate personal style.

    1   2   3   4

3. I am motivated to act as the leader of this group.

    1   2   3   4

4. I am able to adjust my leadership style to meet the developmental needs of the group at a particular point in time.

    1   2   3   4

5. With a Stage 1 group, I am a directive and confident leader.

    1   2   3   4

6. I come to early group meetings with a clear, written agenda.

    1   2   3   4

7. At early meetings, I am able to state the group's goals clearly.

    1   2   3   4

8. Especially in the beginning, I run meetings efficiently.

    1   2   3   4

9. Early on, I am comfortable assigning tasks to individuals as necessary.

    1   2   3   4

10. Early on, I am comfortable making decisions as needed.

    1   2   3   4

11. In early meetings, I work to reduce member anxiety, fears of rejection, and concerns about safety.

$$1 \quad 2 \quad 3 \quad 4$$

12. I treat members sensitively and fairly.

$$1 \quad 2 \quad 3 \quad 4$$

13. I address members by name and make sure members know each others' names from the beginning.

$$1 \quad 2 \quad 3 \quad 4$$

14. I try not to put individuals on the spot, especially in early meetings.

$$1 \quad 2 \quad 3 \quad 4$$

15. I encourage members to participate, but I don't demand participation.

$$1 \quad 2 \quad 3 \quad 4$$

16. I give lots of positive feedback to the group and to individuals.

$$1 \quad 2 \quad 3 \quad 4$$

17. I facilitate open discussion of group goals, values, and tasks.

$$1 \quad 2 \quad 3 \quad 4$$

18. I encourage the expression of different opinions.

$$1 \quad 2 \quad 3 \quad 4$$

19. When members are having difficulty expressing different opinions, I use methods to elicit their opinions anonymously.

$$1 \quad 2 \quad 3 \quad 4$$

20. I facilitate member feelings of competence by providing supervision, training, and education in task-related activities when necessary.

$$1 \quad 2 \quad 3 \quad 4$$

21. I facilitate member feelings of competence by providing supervision, training, and education in group participation skills when necessary.

$$1 \quad 2 \quad 3 \quad 4$$

22. I set high performance standards from the beginning.

$$1 \quad 2 \quad 3 \quad 4$$

23. I review quality expectations early and often.

    1   2   3   4

24. I review standards for member and leader participation as well.

    1   2   3   4

25. Initially, I negotiate with other groups and external individuals for needed resources.

    1   2   3   4

26. Initially, I buffer the group from excessive external demands.

    1   2   3   4

27. Initially, I scan the rest of the organization to collect information that might be useful to the group.

    1   2   3   4

28. Initially, I report group progress to others to ensure that the rest of the organization has a positive image of the group.

    1   2   3   4

29. When members begin to demand more participation in running the group, I slowly begin to empower them to take it.

    1   2   3   4

30. I expect challenges to my authority and see them as a sign of group progress.

    1   2   3   4

31. I try not to take attacks and challenges personally.

    1   2   3   4

32. I facilitate open discussion and resolution of conflicts that emerge.

    1   2   3   4

33. I encourage the use of effective conflict resolution strategies.

    1   2   3   4

34. As the group matures, I increasingly involve members in the leadership function of the group.

    1   2   3   4

35. I encourage and support member efforts to share in the leadership function of the group.

1   2   3   4

36. I encourage the group to make any necessary changes in the group's structure that will facilitate group productivity.

1   2   3   4

37. When a team is fully functional, I act more as an expert member than as a leader.

1   2   3   4

38. I continue to monitor team processes, especially for signs of regression.

1   2   3   4

39. I ask for organizational support reviews on a regular basis.

1   2   3   4

40. Regardless of the stage of the group, I follow the guidelines for effective group membership as well as the guidelines for effective leadership.

1   2   3   4

Minimum Score: 40

Maximum Score: 160

My Score:_____

CHAPTER 7

Navigating Stage 1

Goals of Stage 1

There are certain behaviors that are characteristic of all beginning, or Stage 1, groups. These behaviors can be classified into three categories: concerns about safety and inclusion, member dependency on the designated leader, and a wish for order and structure. Because these categories of behavior happen in all groups during the *Dependency and Inclusion* stage, there must be a reason, or purpose, for their occurrence. If the overall goal of group development is to create an organized unit capable of working effectively and productively to achieve specific ends, then each stage of group development contributes to that overall goal in some way. In order to achieve that overall goal, the first step is to create a sense of belonging and the beginnings of predictable patterns of interaction. That is the purpose of Stage 1.

By the end of Stage 1, members should feel a sense of loyalty to the group. They should want to belong to the group, and they should feel safe enough to contribute ideas and suggestions that will, in their opinion, help the group to achieve its overall objectives. If they don't, the group is likely either to disintegrate or stagnate. Groups disintegrate when members stop attending meetings or participating in group-related activities between meetings. Groups stagnate when the neophyte group system fails to grow and mature.

This chapter briefly describes some typical events that happen during Stage 1 and what members and leaders can do to increase the likelihood that the group members will emerge from Stage 1 with a sense of belonging and a feeling of safety. Also, through the efforts of members and leaders, the group will have developed rudimentary structures that provide an initial sense of order and predictability.

Concerns About Safety and Inclusion

The behaviors, feelings, and attitudes that members of new groups express can be summarized as follows:

- Members are concerned with personal safety in the group.
- Members want to be accepted by other members and the leader.
- Members fear rejection.
- Members communicate in tentative and very polite ways.

An example of how concerns for safety and inclusion might occur in a new group is provided next.

You have been assigned to work on a new group. The first meeting is to be held at 10 o'clock. People begin to arrive a few minutes before 10. You have decided to check things out during this meeting. After all, you know only two other people in the room. You smile at a few people and they smile back but there's not much talking going on. You feel a little awkward, and it's obvious that others do, too. A brave soul asks the person sitting next to him what the purpose of this team is going to be. She shrugs her shoulders in response. A couple of other folks smile and giggle a bit. Someone says, "Adam told me something about it but I'm not very clear. He just said that he was putting a group together to work on a new project and he wanted me on the team." Another person says, "That's how it was with me, too." Others nod in agreement and the room falls silent again.

—— **What You Can Do**

Now that you know that one of the goals of the first stage of group development is to create a sense of safety and inclusion, there are some things that you could do in a situation like this one that could help the group achieve that goal. You could, for example, introduce yourself to the person next to you and talk about what you do in the organization. If you do this loudly enough, others may introduce themselves as well. If not, ask other people who they are.

When the room falls silent, you could comment on how first meetings are always a little awkward but it usually gets better pretty quickly. Statements like these tend to make others feel more comfortable and stimulate further conversation. The key is to keep the goal in mind (safety and inclusion) and act in ways that increase the likelihood of achieving that goal. Don't wait for others to act. Don't wait for the leader to act. Remember that everyone is responsible for the achievement of group goals. So, just do it.

Dependency on the Designated Leader

- The members express a need for dependable and directive leadership.
- The leader is seen as benevolent and competent.
- The leader is expected and encouraged to provide members with direction and personal safety.
- The leader is very rarely challenged.
- Cohesion and commitment to the group is based on identification with the leader.

An example of how these issues might occur in a new group is provided next.

After a few minutes, Adam arrives. He stops to greet a few people as he walks into the room. Everyone seems grateful for his arrival. You think to yourself that Adam is the designated leader of this new group and he will get the ball rolling. Just his arrival seems to have made a difference. Peo-

ple seem more relaxed already. They are all looking at Adam, smiling, and waiting for him to speak.

Adam doesn't waste any time. He doesn't even ask people to introduce themselves. Since he knows everyone, he assumes that others know each other as well. Instead, he begins to outline the tasks of the group and the time line in which tasks have to be accomplished. Some people begin to look a little confused, and others seem a bit tense. No one says anything, though.

— What You Can Do

At this point in time, dependence on the leader is normal. Members expect Adam to take charge. You don't want to undermine Adam's authority or credibility at this point, but you do want to help him do a good job. Adam has forgotten to do a few things. In the best of all possible worlds, Adam would have introduced himself and asked others to do the same. He would have stated the agenda of the meeting and handed out copies of that agenda. He would have stated the goal of the group and launched a discussion about that goal.

If you are the leader of a new group, don't make Adam's mistakes. Come to the meeting prepared. Make sure that people are introduced in enough depth so that they learn not just each others' names but also what people do and what they do well. Provide a detailed agenda that includes a written statement of the group's goal. Spend the first meeting discussing that goal.

Since Adam forgot to do those things, you could help him and the group by asking Adam for introductions. It helps to say something like, "Adam, I may be the only one, but I don't know everybody. Can we introduce ourselves before we get started?"

In a similar fashion, you might ask what the agenda of the meeting is and for clarification of the group's goal. Usually, you won't have to ask all these questions. Others will chime in once the ice is broken. The key is to keep this goal in mind as well. At this point, the group needs a dependable, directive, and competent leader. Help Adam to meet that group need.

If you are the leader, and members ask questions, make suggestions, or point out things that you may have forgotten to do, thank them for their help. Don't get defensive or embarrassed even if a member says something in a way that seems rude or challenging. Assume that group members are trying to be helpful and encourage them to participate. In the long run, you'll be happy that you did.

Some groups don't have designated leaders. This can be a problem that can slow group progress. If this is the case in your group, suggest that a group coordinator be chosen. Some research suggests that leaderless groups have more difficulty getting organized and more difficulty progressing through the stages of group development.

Wish for Order and Structure

- Goals are not clear to members, but clarification is not sought.
- Members rarely express disagreement with initial group goals.
- The group assumes that consensus about goals exists.
- Role assignments tend to be based on external status, first impressions, and initial self-presentation rather than on matching member competencies with goal and task requirements.
- Member compliance is high.
- Communication tends to go through the leader.
- Participation is generally limited to a few vocal members.
- Conflict is minimal.
- Conformity is high.
- A lack of group structure and organization is evident.
- Member deviation from emerging norms is rare.
- Subgroups and coalitions are rare at this stage.

An example of how these issues might occur in a new group is provided next.

Adam responds to your request and states the goal of the group. He asks if people are clear about the goal and everyone nods. You remain a little confused by the goal but, because everyone seems to understand what's expected, you don't say anything. Next, Adam returns to outlining the tasks of the group and the time line in which tasks have to be accomplished. He asks for volunteers to take on the various tasks.

BOX 7.1
Best Excuse

This group ran the company. The members were the senior vice presidents and the CEO. I was going over the results of a group assessment that I had done with them. The group was stuck in Stage 1. While they knew that they disagreed about many things, no one was willing to raise controversial issues. In fact, many members did not talk very much at meetings. I said that things would not change unless they began to discuss these things. The CEO said, "Oh, we forgot to tell you that we took the Myers-Briggs test and all of us scored high on introversion. We're all introverts." I replied, "I don't care if you're aardvarks. You guys run the show. Your cars cost more than many people's homes. You have to talk to each other."

— What You Can Do

From reading this book, you know that if goals are not perfectly clear and accepted by everybody, the chances of group success are limited. You also know that planning how to accomplish tasks and discussing who should do each task also is crucial to group success. Finally, you know that ensuring that input is sought from all group members increases the chances of group success. So, you ask Adam and the group to discuss their understanding of the goal in a little more depth. Later, you raise the issue of role assignments. It's best to raise this issue by inquiring about your own role, especially if it doesn't seem appropriate to you based on your skills and abilities. Of course, chances are slim that you will have to raise all these issues. By now, other members will be raising issues as well.

A word of advice for leaders is in order here. You also know that discussing goals at length, spending time planning how to accomplish tasks, and assigning tasks based on member skills is important to group success. Make sure these things happen, but don't hog the limelight too much. Members raising issues, rather than you raising those issues, is a good thing. Don't be too perfect and don't be too dominant. Provide for member safety. Provide initial direction and support member attempts to participate.

This chapter has provided some examples of events that typically occur in Stage 1 groups. It was not meant to cover all possible scenarios. The real intention of this chapter and those that follow is to help members and leaders develop a framework to guide their actions in groups. The framework is pretty simple. Know the goals of each stage of development and act in ways that will help your group achieve those goals. If the members and leaders described in this chapter follow that advice, the group will move forward. People will develop a sense of belonging and safety, members will begin to trust Adam's leadership skills, and the beginnings of order will appear. The group will be ready to move on.

CHAPTER 8

Surviving Stage 2

Goals of Stage 2

Having safely navigated the first stage of group development, members and the leader have developed an initial sense of loyalty to the group. Some degree of organization has begun to emerge, and people feel safer to express themselves in the group. Now, some hard work has to be done. If the group is to become a unit capable of performing at high levels, then both members and the leader need to create a unified group culture and an effective group organizational structure in which to work.

Group culture refers to a set of shared perceptions or assumptions about values, norms, and goals. These assumptions, once established, dictate how people will behave and the kind of organizational structure the group will require in order to express its cultural assumptions and achieve its goals.

In the first stage of group development, members were primarily concerned with personal safety and feeling included. Preliminary discussions probably occurred about how people should interact in the group and how members should organize themselves to accomplish tasks. More discussions will be needed, however, to reach agreement about these things. The participation of every member also will be required for this to occur.

The second stage of group development is described as a period of *Counterdependency and Fight.* This is so because conflict with the leader and among group members is inevitable if the goals of Stage 2 are to be reached. The group's goal at this stage is to develop a unified set of goals, values, and operational procedures, and this goal usually generates conflict. Differences of opinion are very likely to occur. Conflict is also necessary for the establishment of trust and a climate in which members feel free to disagree with each other.

Some groups become mired in conflict and remain stuck at this developmental stage. Other groups are overwhelmed by the stress of this phase and revert to leader dependence in an attempt to avoid further conflict. Neither of these outcomes has positive effects for the group or for the quality of work that will be generated by the group. Only through conflict resolution and the development of a unified view of the group's purpose and processes can true collaboration be achieved.

This chapter briefly describes some typical events that happen during Stage 2 and what members and leaders can do to increase the likelihood that group members will emerge from this stage with a shared culture and an organizational structure that will enable them to be productive and successful. It also describes how working to achieve the goals of Stage 2 increases trust among group members and makes working together more enjoyable as well as more effective.

Create a Unified Group Culture

The first thing a group needs to do during Stage 2 is to begin to create a unified group culture. Here are some things that will happen as a group attempts to do this:

- Conflicts about values emerge.
- Disagreements about goals and tasks emerge.
- Increased feelings of safety allow dissent to occur.
- Members challenge the leader and each other.
- Clarification of goals begins.
- Decreased conformity begins.
- Deviation from emerging group norms beings to occur.

Some examples of how these issues might occur in a Stage 2 group are provided next.

The group has been meeting for about 8 weeks. Nina, the group's leader, is going over a list of things that the group needs to work on in the coming weeks if they are to stay on schedule. Suddenly, Jack says, "I'm not sure about this, Nina. How can they expect us to come up with such a complicated policy in such a short period of time? I'm not even sure that a policy will solve this problem. I'm not convinced that this is the right way to go." A few other members nod their heads in agreement with Jack.

Nina is stunned. She thought that members had agreed to the group's goal weeks ago. She wonders if this is just a power play on Jack's part or if he really means it.

— What You Can Do

This kind of situation occurs quite often in Stage 2 groups. When people say that the group seems to be going in circles or rehashing topics that already have been discussed and resolved, it is usually due to situations like this one. People are in a hurry to get on with things. They easily get upset with members who revisit issues that they think have been decided already.

Instead of getting frustrated or angry at an individual or two, try to remember two things. First, remember that when things were initially discussed, the group was in Stage 1. Some people did not feel safe enough to express disagreement at that point. It seemed like everyone agreed, but not everyone expressed his or her opinion. Later on, when feelings of safety have increased, disagreements get voiced. This is a good thing.

Second, when a group is faced with a complicated set of goals and tasks, it takes people some time to examine those goals and tasks thoroughly. Forming opinions about things does not happen quickly, especially if those opinions are important to individual and group success. It's a good thing to revisit issues after members have had time to think. It's a very good thing, actually. Many decisions or agreements made in haste have been the wrong ones.

It would help the group if you said something like, "I'm glad that Jack brought this up. It makes a lot of sense to discuss our goals and objectives again to make sure that everybody's on the same page." Whether you are a member or the leader of this group, this would be a very helpful thing to say. It may be harder for Nina, or any leader, to say it since she may think that Jack's comments were meant as an attack on her leadership. It would be wise of her to say it anyway. If Nina doesn't say it, a member should try to ward off a potentially negative argument between these two people. The issue isn't whether Jack is trying to undermine Nina's authority. He may or may not be doing that. It doesn't matter. What matters for the group at this stage in its development is to make sure that everyone agrees with, and understands, the group's goal.

The group had developed the habit of holding lunch meetings. Jane didn't like this, since she usually worked out at the company's gym during lunch. She skipped a meeting and went to the gym. Other members were appalled and confronted her about her lack of commitment to the group at the next meeting. Jane said that she didn't like the meeting time because it infringed on her personal time. She even said that she bet that some other people were unhappy with the meeting time, too. A couple of people said they agreed with Jane. Some people just shook their heads.

— What You Can Do

During Stage 1, many norms get established without much discussion. In this case, it is likely that meeting during lunch worked well for the group leader. In Stage 1, people tend to go along with whatever the leader proposes. So, lunchtime meetings became the norm. As the group developed, and people began to feel more comfortable with each other, those who didn't like the meeting time became more vocal. This, too, is a good thing.

If group norms undermine people's motivation to attend or participate in the group, changes are in order. Finding a mutually agreeable meeting time is challenging in the busy workplace. It's important, though. If members skip meetings, the effects on the group will be negative. A large part of each meeting will be devoted to catching people up on what occurred at the last meeting. This will slow down or stop group progress. If people attend but are resentful of the meeting time, they will not participate fully and may act in unproductive ways.

If a situation like this occurs in your group, it would be helpful to say something like, "I think we should try to find a meeting time that fits everyone's schedule. How's Tuesday at 3?"

Many norms emerge during the first stage of group development that will be challenged in the second stage. As this example shows:

Lora tends to go on and on at meetings. Whatever the topic, she has an opinion, which she expresses in great detail. You want to express an opinion as well and you know that other people would like to air their views. No one interrupts Lora, however. They just sit and fidget or stare straight ahead. No one feels that they can give feedback to others about their group behavior. Although it's never been voiced, everyone knows that giving feedback violates some unstated rule. Members feel that they have to be nice and that they have to be tolerant in this group.

— What You Can Do

Generally speaking, being nice and tolerant of others is a good norm to establish. If that means that the group will fail to achieve its work goals, however, then the norm is too strict and should be altered. As people begin to feel safer, voicing disagreement with norms and suggesting elimination or alteration of some norms will occur. In fact, it must occur if the group is going to develop a culture that will support group goal achievement.

In this case, you could say something like the following: "Lora, I think I understand your position on this and I want to hear from others as well before I make up my mind. What do the rest of you think about this?" You'll probably feel a little uncomfortable doing this because you're breaking a group rule. Keep in mind, though, that if Lora is allowed to monopolize the conversation for much longer, the frustrations of others will continue to mount. Eventually, someone (maybe even you) will explode and confront Lora in a very negative way. The confrontation may get very personal and precipitate a feud in the group. Some members will rush to Lora's defense, and others may join the attack against Lora. This will not only be a colossal waste of group time, but will be very hurtful to Lora and to group morale. It's better to intervene early in a situation like this. Do so with all the diplomacy and tact you can muster. Be gentle. Don't blame Lora for her behavior. Focus on what the group needs to do in order to accomplish its goals.

These examples emphasize two important things about norms. First, don't make norms about unimportant things. Adopting too many norms is like having too many laws in a society. If every aspect of group life is legislated, people feel constrained. They won't feel free to express themselves, which seriously limits input and creativity. Ultimately, this will decrease the chances of group success.

Second, scrutinize norms for their contribution to group effectiveness and productivity. If they don't measure up, eliminate or modify them. Norms are necessary to create predictable patterns of behavior and similarity in member values and attitudes. They must relate to goals and objectives, however. If norms interfere with achievement and high performance, change them.

Gordon, the leader of the group, has just laid out his plan to increase sales in a specific region. Walter, the sales director in that region, reacts by saying, "You just don't get it, Gordon. What you're proposing won't work in a million years! If you had any sense of the history of this problem or the people in my region, you'd know that. When was the last time you met with us? Was it two or three years ago?"

— What You Can Do

This is one of the scarier moments in group life. A member has attacked the leader in a very personal and confrontational way. This kind of confrontation does not always happen. In groups that ultimately are successful, disagreements with the leader happen quite a lot. Generally, however, the disagreements are milder, more tactfully phrased, and do not challenge the leader's competence or intelligence.

Challenging the leader is an essential part of group life. If group members always accept the leader's views, there is no reason to have a group at all. A major reason for working in groups is the assumption that decisions made by groups will be better than those of the best and brightest group member alone. That is, collective intelligence is assumed to be greater than individual intelligence. While I am not sure that this always is the case, it is the case in a high performance team. To become a high performance team, however, and to utilize collective intelligence, the dominance of the leader must be reduced so that others can contribute to that collective intelligence. Disagreements with leaders are necessary at times in order to produce the best decisions and to achieve at high levels.

Obviously, how one disagrees with a leader, or a member, for that matter, is key. In the current example, Walter not only disagrees with Gordon's plan, he also challenges Gordon personally. He chastises Gordon for his lack of knowledge about the region and for his lack of attention to regional problems. This type of conflict can be very destructive to a group. Some members will be frightened by this situation. Feelings of safety, so essential to group unity, will be undermined, and some members may retreat into silence. Other members may jump to Gordon's defense. Still others may side with Walter in opposition to Gordon. This could lead to an irreparable split in the group. It could spell doom for the group if the split cannot be repaired.

You must act quickly to keep these things from happening. Keep a few things in mind as you do this. First, in all likelihood, Gordon is hurt and angry because of what Walter has said. He also may be embarrassed by this public challenge to his leadership and will want to save face. Walter probably is feeling angry, a little embarrassed about his outburst, and anxious about what Gordon will do in response. You should proceed with caution in this emotional situation. You should act, however, because this situation could have very negative effects on the group.

Say something like the following: "I know what it's like to feel loyal to the people back home, Walter. It's hard for any of us to know what really is going on there. All of us, including Gordon, want you to lay out your plans to increase sales. Maybe some others have ideas to contribute, too. Is that okay with everybody?"

Your intention in making this, or a similar statement, is to refocus the group on developing a plan to increase sales and to defuse the tension between Gordon and Walter. If your intervention works, the focus will return to the task at hand. You will probably get a lot of help from other group members once you say this. Other members will be eager to reduce the mounting tension.

Earlier in this book, I talked about how important it is to avoid getting involved in personality conflicts and personal fights. This example makes clear why this is so important. Nothing threatens group success more than destructive personal arguments.

If you find yourself in a position similar to Walter's, don't do what he did. If Walter had said the following, this whole situation could have been avoided: "I see what your plan is based on, Gordon, but I want to update you on some current issues in the region. Some things have happened that you may not be aware of."

If you find yourself in Gordon's situation someday, and someone like Walter challenges you in a negative way, remember that a leader's job is to work for the good of the group. It would be in the group's best interest for you to say "You're right, Walter, I may not be aware of some recent developments. Tell me what's been going on lately." This is not easy to do when you are feeling unduly attacked. It's not easy to stifle your urge to retaliate. No one said leadership was easy, however. Do what's best for the group.

Create a Unified and Effective Group Structure

As Stage 2 groups begin to create an effective group structure, the following things are likely to occur:

- Dissatisfaction with roles may surface.
- Role clarification also begins.
- Disagreements about strategies to accomplish group tasks begin to surface.
- Disagreements about how to make decisions also may emerge.
- Subgroups and coalitions form.
- Group intolerance of subgroups, cliques, and coalitions is evident.
- Increased member participation is evident.
- Attempts at conflict management begin.
- Increased consensus about group goals and culture become evident near the end of this stage.
- Conflict resolution, if successful, increases trust and cohesion.

Some examples of how these issues might occur in a Stage 2 group are provided next.

In one of the early meetings, Penny, the group leader, asked you to investigate the budget implications of increasing the sales force in a certain area. At the time, you agreed to do it. After a while, you began to feel uncomfortable with the assignment because you're unfamiliar with the product line in that area. You believe that Jean would do a better job but don't know how to bring this up.

— What You Can Do

Perhaps the best way to handle this situation is to approach Penny outside the meeting and say something like this: "I'm feeling a little queasy about my assignment. Jean is more familiar with the product line in that area than I am. She might do a better job. I think she's working on getting the figures for the ad campaign. I'm pretty up on that. Maybe we could switch? If you think it's a good idea, we could suggest a switch at the next meeting."

If the role you are in doesn't match your abilities and talents, try to negotiate for one that does. In the long run, the group will benefit from having the right people in the right roles. Don't avoid challenges, though. Another way to deal with this might be to team up with Jean to work on your assignment. You might learn a lot that way. Whether you switch with or team up with Jean should depend on the group's needs. If time is of the essence, switching is probably best. If developing group members with multiple skills is important to group success, working with Jean on the assignment might be best.

The group is discussing what to do about a particularly difficult decision it must make. Mary breaks into the conversation and says, "I thought we decided this last week. Doesn't anybody else remember that? This happens all the time. We keep revisiting our decisions. They never seem to stick. No wonder we're behind schedule."

— What You Can Do

This is a common situation in groups. Typically, the reason for this is that the group has developed a very informal decision-making process. Sometimes, it's so informal that some members don't even know when a decision is being made. There was a time when minutes were taken at every group meeting. There also was a time when votes were taken and members raised their hands to signify their position. Over the years, such practices have been abandoned in favor of more informal meeting procedures. The results of this informality are not always positive. Groups need clear decision-making processes that members accept. How groups make decisions may vary. There is no best decision-making process that should be used in all cases. Regardless of which decision-making process is chosen, however, members and the leader should agree to that process in advance.

In this case, an informal process has been enacted and I would bet that this was done with no discussion. Like many other aspects of group structure, it just happened without much thought or discussion. What you could do to help in this situation might be to say something like, "I remember, Mary, but some other people don't. That worries me. Maybe we should make a list of recent decisions we've made to see what we all remember. It also might be a good idea to talk about how we want to make decisions and whether we should record the decisions that we make."

In an effort to get tasks done faster, group members have decided to delegate some tasks to a subgroup of 3 members. These 3 are to report back to the group when they have finished. Lately, however, some other members have become a little irritated and suspicious of members of the subgroup. They wonder what they're doing and seem to feel excluded by them. They even seem to resent the fact that "The Group of Three" tends to talk with each other more than with the rest of the members.

— What You Can Do

Establishing subgroups is a logical way to increase group output and task performance. Division of labor is necessary whenever complex tasks need to be completed in a timely manner. Logical though it may be, it usually is perceived by others as a threat to group unity and cohesion. This is a normal human response. Remember how it felt in high school when you were not invited to join a popular clique? Even if you didn't really want to be a part of that group, it didn't feel good to be excluded. We may be all grown up, but some of those feelings remain. Most people want to be "in on things." We want to know what others are doing. We want to belong.

In a Stage 2 group, trust is just beginning to build. Members have not developed enough faith in the trustworthiness of their colleagues to be certain that a subset of them would work for the good of the whole group. Maybe they are looking out for themselves or talking about other members in their private meetings. While this may sound paranoid, human beings do have a bit of a paranoid streak.

There are two options in situations like this. The group could choose not to employ subgroups to accomplish tasks or members could use the emergence of subgroups as an opportunity to increase group trust and cohesion. Obviously, I endorse the latter. The emergence of subgroups is very important to group effectiveness. It's a sign that the group is getting organized, and an organized group is much more likely to be successful. Learning to tolerate and to trust subgroups, then, is vital to group success.

If you are not a member of the subgroup and you have noticed that other nonmembers (perhaps yourself included) are uncomfortable with subgroup members, you might say something like the following: "We're not very comfortable yet with delegating tasks to subgroups. Maybe it would help if the subgroups that we created reported more frequently about what they're working on. That might help them stay on track and help the rest of us feel more comfortable. It also would give the subgroup members the opportunity to get some input from us and give us some ideas as well."

If you are a member of the subgroup and you have noticed that others seem a bit uncomfortable with you, you could raise the same issue by saying, "The three of us have been thinking that we'd like to keep you up to date about what we're doing. Could we get 5 minutes on the agenda to fill you in and ask for advice if we need it?"

Also, if you are a member of a subgroup, keep your commitments. If you are to report back to the whole group on a given date, do so. This is always important to do, but especially important for the first few subgroups. If those early subgroups keep other members and leaders informed of their progress and keep their commitments, group trust and cohesion will increase significantly.

Marie and Tim are arguing about the best way to raise money for the new wing of the museum. Grants and state funding will provide 60% of what's needed. The museum staff must raise the rest. Each believes that her or his

---

BOX 8.1
Holy War

An interfaith group of priests, nuns, and ministers were in conflict. The male priests and ministers blamed the nuns for the group's problems. They accused the nuns of being too enamored of discussion and dialogue. The men felt that all this talk was going nowhere. After working with this group for a while, it became clear that the real problem was that the group did not have a clear decision-making procedure. Once a decision-making procedure was in place, peace was restored.

---

way will raise the most money in the shortest time. The rest of the staff has taken sides, and the disagreement is pretty intense.

— What You Can Do

Conflict resolution is an essential component of group success. If this becomes a long, drawn-out disagreement, nobody benefits. You can help in this situation by saying something like this: "Let's stop for a minute and outline both plans in detail. Then we can see what we're really talking about in terms of investment of money and staff time. Who knows? Maybe there's a way to combine aspects of both plans. We won't know that, though, until we go over each plan in detail. What do the rest of you think?"

The second stage of group development can be difficult. The goals of this stage are not easy. On U.S. coins is the phrase *e pluribus unum,* which means "from many, one." From many individuals with many points of view, one group must be forged with a coherent culture and structure that will facilitate goal achievement. This is no easy task, but it is made less difficult if members know what to expect and how to help each other accomplish it.

Reorganizing at Stage 3

Goals of Stage 3

If a group manages to work through the inevitable conflicts of Stage 2, member trust, commitment to the group, and willingness to cooperate increase. Communication becomes more open and task oriented. Members focus more on the task and less on issues of status, power, or influence. This third stage of group development, referred to as the *Trust and Structure* phase, is characterized by more mature negotiations about roles, organization, and procedures. It is also a time in which members work to solidify positive relationships with each other.

Some things that happen during Stage 3 are described next.

Fine-Tuning Roles, Organization, and Procedures

In the process of fine-tuning roles, the level of organization and group procedures, the following things are likely to occur:

- Increased goal clarity and consensus are evident.
- Roles and tasks are adjusted to increase the likelihood of goal achievement.

- The leader's role becomes less directive and more consultative.
- The communication structure becomes more flexible.
- The content of communication becomes more task oriented.
- Increased tolerance of subgroups, cliques, and coalitions is evident.
- Greater division of labor occurs.
- Conflict continues to occur, but it is managed more effectively.

Some examples of how these issues might occur in a Stage 3 group are provided next.

Phyllis, the group's leader, is actively engaged in the group's discussion. A member named John is running the meeting. Phyllis brings up some new ideas but, after some discussion, the group decides to go with another plan. Then the group runs into a snag. Members are unsure how to implement the plan. Everyone turns to Phyllis for her input.

— What You Can Do

At the third stage of group development, leaders are not as prominent as they were in earlier stages. By this time, members are beginning to take over some leadership functions. In this example, a member is running the meeting, which allows the leader to participate more actively in the discussion. Members are much more comfortable with and, in general, less dependent on the leader for direction. This way of operating is new for the group, however, and there will be moments when the group may revert to previous ways of behaving. In this case, when the group could not reach a decision, members looked to the leader for direction.

This situation is very normal and quite common. Development does not proceed in one direction. We often take two steps forward and one step back. The members and the leader should be mindful of this tendency but not overly concerned. On the other hand, members and leaders should strive to support forward motion. If Phyllis makes this decision for the group, it will not be the end of the world, but it may slow progress a little bit.

If you are a member of the group, you could help by saying something like, "Hey, let's try to resolve this issue as a group. There's no need to put this on Phyllis. We've dealt with tougher issues than this before." Obviously, you should make this statement with good humor and a smile.

If you are Phyllis, you may feel the urge to "save the group" by making the decision. Try to resist that urge. It would probably be best to say something like, "I'm not sure what we should do. Let's discuss this a while longer and see what we come up with."

Todd just came back from a fishing trip. He is telling "fish stories" that are pretty funny. Everyone is enjoying listening to him. He's been talking for about 5 minutes and the meeting is scheduled to last for 1 hour. There are a number of issues that must be dealt with in that hour.

— What You Can Do

Having a bit of fun at a meeting is a positive thing and a sign that people are comfortable with each other. It reduces stress and can increase feelings of cohesion. When the fun goes on too long, however, productivity may be compromised. In a Stage 3 group, members are very interested in work. Their conversations are more task oriented and everyone is interested in being efficient and productive. The group is not a high performance team yet, but members want the group to reach high levels of productivity.

There is nothing inherently wrong with Todd's fish stories. However, if you are beginning to worry about getting work done, or if you sense that others are, you might say, "Todd, these stories are wonderful but it's time for us to get to work."

Annette has just returned from a meeting with Nancy, the vice president, and other project leaders. She reports the details of the meeting to the group members. She's a little worried because two coordinating groups are being set up to oversee aspects of the overall contract. Annette feels stretched to the max and says, "I don't know how I can attend all these meetings, get my other work done, and be responsible to the group."

— What You Can Do

One of the hallmarks of a Stage 3 group is that members begin to take on aspects of the leadership role. One important aspect of that role is to communicate and negotiate with other parts of the organization. Groups can lose their way if members don't maintain open communications with other groups that are relevant to their success.

In today's workplace, everyone is busy. Most people that I run into feel overloaded. Interacting with other relevant groups, however, is important to group success. You could help by saying something like, "Annette, maybe a few of us could represent our group at those meetings. Someone needs to go, but I don't think it has to be you."

Solidifying Positive Relationships

In the process of building positive relationships among group members, the following things are likely to occur:

- Cohesion and trust increase.
- Member satisfaction also increases.
- Cooperation is more evident.
- Individual commitment to group goals and tasks is high.
- Voluntary conformity with group norms increases.
- Helpful deviation is tolerated.

Some examples of how these things occur in Stage 3 groups are provided next.

Al is an odd duck. He doesn't say much during meetings and seems to spend his time doodling on a notepad. For the first few months, group members were uncomfortable with Al and rarely asked for his opinion. After all, he didn't seem to care enough to participate. Every once in a while, though, Al would say something that was right on and very helpful. When it comes to engine design, he really knows his stuff.

— What You Can Do

This group has developed a strong norm for participation, and that is a very good thing. It's difficult to develop a high performance team without the participation of the majority of members. For whatever reasons, Al is not a talker. This makes others uncomfortable with him, and they question his commitment to the group. They don't perceive him as a team player. On the other hand, when Al does say something, it's worth listening to him. What he does say is usually very helpful.

Ignoring Al or insisting that he become a more active participant will not help the situation. Al is Al, after all. You could help by noticing the kinds of input that Al contributes and when those topics come up, asking Al for his thoughts. You could say, "Al knows more about this than any of us. Can you help us out with this, Al?"

People are different. Some of us are talkers and some of us are not. Some of us follow rules and norms to the letter. Some of us don't. As long as people are making a positive contribution to the group, however small, let them be. The workplace values conformity and some degree of conformity is necessary if groups are to be successful, but too much conformity can be a negative. If we are all behaving and thinking in the same way, generating new ideas may be difficult. Sometimes, oddball ideas are the best ideas.

Some people in the group are expressing concern about whether Colleen, Barbara, and Chris will finish their report in time. They didn't come to the meeting today and no one knows why.

— What You Can Do

By the third stage of group development, trust is pretty high. There will be moments, however, when feelings of mistrust will surface. This is natural, especially when time is of the essence. You know that people like Colleen, Barbara, and Chris. They're just worried about staying on schedule.

You could help by saying something like, "Colleen, Barbara, and Chris will get it done. They're as worried about deadlines as we are. They may need some help, though. I'd be willing to check in with them this week and offer a hand if they need it."

Brigid was asked by the group to fill in the details of a new insurance product that members are considering. She's been working on it for 2

BOX 9.1
Strangest Goal

I asked a team what their goal was, and they said, in unison, "To be a cohesive team." I asked them if the company paid them well for their efforts.

---

weeks. At the meeting, Brigid says, "I've got most of the details worked out, but a few things have me stumped. I could use some help."

— What You Can Do

In the competitive world of business, asking for help is not easy. The fact that Brigid asked for help is a sign that she trusts other group members and that she is committed to doing the best possible job. This is terrific and should be encouraged.

You could help by saying something like, "Can you tell us what's got you stumped? I'm sure one of us could help. If not, someone probably knows who to go to for the answers."

The third stage of group development is a time when group processes and procedures are adjusted so that the group can work at higher levels of performance. Some issues already were resolved at Stage 2, but other norms, strategies, and roles need to be scrutinized to ensure that they contribute to group goal achievement.

Now that group members have resolved many earlier issues, trust has increased. Members feel comfortable enough to question how the group is functioning and to suggest changes to increase the chances of success. It's a time to get organized and to plan better ways of working together. It's also the time to solidify working relationships among members.

One word of caution is necessary here. Some groups enter Stage 3 and focus too much energy on building relationships and not enough on getting organized. These groups begin to resemble "love-ins" after a while. They are so busy supporting each other that they forget to make sure that how they are working together is the best way. Remember that research sug-

gests that about 15% to 20% of group time should be focused on supporting each other. The rest should be focused on work as much as possible.

Other groups focus too much energy on getting organized and forget
to support and encourage each other in that endeavor. That is a classic
formula for burnout. If members don't feel supported by the group and
others external to the group, they will become disillusioned and resentful.
If that happens, the group will find itself back at Stage 2 in a flash.

CHAPTER 10

Sustaining High Performance

Goals of Stage 4

As its name implies, the fourth, or *Work,* stage of group development is a time of intense productivity and effectiveness. It is at this stage that a work group becomes a team. Having resolved many of the issues of the previous stages, the team can focus most of its energy on goal achievement and task accomplishment. Although work occurs at every developmental stage, the quality and quantity of work increase significantly during Stage 4.

The goals of Stage 4 include getting the work done well, making decisions, remaining cohesive while encouraging task-related conflicts, and maintaining high performance over the long haul.

Sadly, many people have never participated on a Stage 4 team. They don't know what it's like to work at high performance levels and to enjoy the experience. Some teams that make it to Stage 4 contain members for whom this is a new experience. They are excited by the ease with which work gets done. They are thrilled with the feelings of camaraderie and trust generated by the team. They are happy that they are learning so much and are eager for this experience to continue for as long as possible. The problem is, however, that unless members are careful, backsliding may occur.

BOX 10.1
Pride Cometh . . .

Two groups were working on similar projects. They asked for feedback on how they were doing. I assessed both groups and gave them suggestions on how to improve. The Stage 3 group used the feedback and worked hard to improve its performance. The Stage 4 team didn't. They felt they were doing great and would beat the other group easily. They did not.

Getting to Stage 4 is not easy. Many groups never do. Staying at Stage 4 isn't easy, either. Without constant vigilance, teams may regress to earlier stages of development. To maintain high levels of performance for an extended period of time, team members need to learn some things and to do some things that will keep their effectiveness and performance at high levels. Some of the things that high performance teams do to remain effective are described next.

Getting the Work Done Well

The norms in high performance teams support not only getting the work done, but getting the work done well. Those norms include the following:

- Team norms encourage high performance and quality.
- The team expects to be successful.
- The team encourages innovation.
- The team pays attention to the details of its work.

Some examples of how these norms get enacted in high performance teams are provided next.

Felice has just suggested a way to get things done faster by eliminating a few steps where quality checks are made. After all, there are other points in the process where the product quality is checked. She believes this will save valuable time and some money as well. You are not sure that this is a good idea.

— What You Can Do

One of the goals of a Stage 4 team is to get the work done well. Norms for quality and high performance have been established and everyone wants to do the best job possible. You know that Felice does, as well. She also wants to save time and money, which is not a bad idea if it can be done without compromising quality. Felice's idea will save money. There's no doubt of that. You're not so sure how her plan will affect product quality, however.

Given that the goal is to get the work done well, you might say something like, "Felice, I think we should go over your plan very carefully. I'm as eager as you are to save money and time. I just want to make sure that product quality won't be affected."

The point of saying this is to remind everyone of the norm for quality as well as for high performance. As work intensifies and deadlines loom, it's easy to forget commitments to quality. Gentle reminders are very helpful.

Felice agrees with you that quality is important and describes her plan in more detail. She says that there are enough checks at other points in the process to ensure that quality is not compromised. You and other team members are impressed with Felice's careful evaluation of the steps in the process. She really did her homework.

— What You Can Do

Part of getting the job done well is to encourage team members to be innovative. Felice has come up with an innovative idea, and, after a lengthy team discussion, members think that idea is a good one. You might say, "Felice, I didn't understand at first but you've made a believer out of me. I say we go with your idea. What do the rest of you think?"

Renaya is feeling overwhelmed by the team's current workload. She says, "I'm not sure that we can do all this by the end of the month. It seems too much for us to handle."

— What You Can Do

Even members of Stage 4 teams can become anxious about team success. Teams also can set goals for themselves that are too ambitious. The feeling that the team will succeed is vital to high performance. If teams become uncertain about goal achievement, there will be negative repercussions. You want the team to maintain its expectation of success. You also want to address Renaya's concern. You might say, "Renaya, I think we should review our plans for the month. Maybe they are too ambitious. Maybe we haven't divided the workload evenly enough. It could be that you got more than your share. What do the rest of you think about this?"

The team is planning a meeting with the production team to establish the time frame for launching a new product. Dan has been given the responsibility for working out the agenda with George, who heads the production team. Dan has just presented the agenda to the group. Jane says, "Dan, I think that the agenda includes most of what we need to clear up, but I'm a little concerned about coordinating marketing and production time lines. Shouldn't marketing be included in that meeting?"

— What You Can Do

Because paying attention to details is an important component of group success, you might say something like this: "I agree with Jane, Dan. Marketing should be represented at the meeting. I also think it would be a good idea to go over the agenda again to make doubly sure that we've covered everything and have all the right players at the meeting." If you are Dan, don't get defensive. People are not trying to find fault with your work. In Stage 4 teams, everyone is committed to getting the work done well. Reviewing plans and checking things twice are an expression of that commitment.

Making Decisions

Decision making in high performance teams is a careful process that involves the following:

- The team spends time defining problems it must solve or decisions it must make.
- The team spends time planning how it will solve problems and make decisions.
- The team spends enough time discussing problems and decisions that must be solved.
- The team determines methods for decision making that are participatory.
- The team implements and evaluates its solutions and decisions.

Examples of how high performance teams make decisions and what you can do to help are provided next.

Kate says, "Can't we just change the schedule of the show so that it doesn't occur on the same weekend as the Motherwell exhibit at the museum? I don't want our artists to be overshadowed by anything." Mike says, "I agree with you, but I'm worried about what that will do to the whole schedule."

— What You Can Do

The team is about to make a decision. You know that in order to make a good decision the team needs to define the problem clearly. It may seem that the problem is clear. Another institution has scheduled an exhibit that may keep people from attending your institution's art exhibit. Before rearranging your schedule, however, it would make sense to make sure that you have defined the problem correctly. You might say, "You might be right that the Motherwell show will compete with ours. I'd feel better, though, if we talked about that a little more before we start thinking of solutions."

Bunny has a different take on the situation. She thinks that the Motherwell show will attract different people. Midge disagrees. She says, "Motherwell has earned a place in art history. Even people who are not particularly attracted to his work will go to the exhibit because of his stature in contemporary art." Other group members begin to take sides with either Bunny or Midge.

— What You Can Do

Defining problems clearly often requires going beyond the team for information. You might say, "I think we're stuck. We have two different opinions about this. Maybe we should ask some other people for their thoughts on this. Who might know more about this kind of situation than we do?"

Bunny and Midge contact three curators whose institutions had exhibits that were held at the same time as exhibits of well-known figures in the art world. All three said that attendance at their exhibits was higher than expected. People who came from out of town for the major exhibit made the rounds of other art exhibits and shows in the area. Kate remains unconvinced.

— What You Can Do

You might say, "Kate, I think the team is ready to make a decision on this. We usually vote and go with the majority. Since this is really important to you, I think it would be best in this case to try to reach consensus on this decision. Let's discuss all the options again and see if we can come up with a decision that everyone can live with. Is that OK with everybody?"

By suggesting a change in the decision-making process, you are making it clear to everyone that Kate's position has to be taken seriously. It will also remind Kate that the team cares about her and also must take action on this issue. Consensus, in this team, does not mean that everyone has to be enthusiastic about a decision. It simply means that everyone can live with the decision. After further discussion, Kate may still be skeptical, but may be willing to go along with the emerging consensus. She may agree to go along this time as an experiment. It is unlikely that Kate will attempt to block the decision. This team has established a norm that encourages members to go along with decisions as long as the team has done its best to discuss the problem, uncover relevant information, and sought input from all members.

Cohesion and Conflict

Positive relationships are evident in high performance teams. Conflicts continue to occur as well. In high performance teams, the following characteristics are in evidence:

- The team is highly cohesive.
- Interpersonal attraction among members is high.
- Members are cooperative.
- Periods of conflict are frequent but brief.
- The team has effective conflict management strategies.

Some examples of how teams remain cohesive and deal with conflict are provided next.

The team has been thrown a curve ball. The court date has been moved up due to political pressure, and this legal defense team must be prepared for trial much earlier than expected. Members of the team know that there's no chance of getting the date moved back. They'll just have to be ready.

— What You Can Do

You might say something like, "I was planning to go away for the weekend but I'll cancel that. That will give me time to work with Janice on preparing those motions. What do you say, Janice?"

Teams at Stage 4 step up to challenges. The world is not predictable. What's more, it is often stressful. In teams that are functioning well, people make the necessary adjustments in order to get the job done. A word of caution is in order here. If members find themselves in situations like this frequently, it may be a sign that they should review their operational procedures. Too many situations like this one may overload team members and cause burnout. This particular situation seems unavoidable. Others, however, may be avoidable with some forethought.

Bob is getting hot under the collar. He disagrees strongly with Tom's proposed changes in patient education procedures for the unit. "Sure, these changes will save time, but I will not compromise patient care for anybody." Tom is hurt by this statement and says, "I'm not trying to do that. I'm just trying to standardize our approach to patient education. That is what will save the time."

— What You Can Do

You know that conflicts occur at every stage of group development. In fact, conflicts are good since they often help to clarify things. You also know that the way conflicts are handled is critical. So, you say, "This is a very important issue. I think we should take both these points of view very seriously and get other members' opinions as well. In fact, it might be useful to see what other units like ours are doing about patient education. What do the rest of you think?"

By redirecting the conversation away from Bob and Tom and back to the team as a whole, tempers will undoubtedly cool. Both men's concerns have been acknowledged and taken seriously. Other members will have the opportunity to weigh in on these issues, and the idea of seeking information from other hospitals will probably be received positively by team members. The trick in conflict situations is to intervene quickly and stay focused on the task.

Maintaining High Performance

High performance is maintained in Stage 4 in the following ways:

- The team gets, gives, and utilizes feedback about its effectiveness and productivity.
- The team evaluates its performance on a regular basis.
- The team takes steps to avoid routine and getting stuck in a rut.

Some examples of how teams maintain high performance and what you can do to help are provided next.

John is facilitating this meeting. The team rotates the job of meeting facilitator, which gives Joyce, the designated leader, the chance to participate more fully in discussions. Halfway through the meeting, John says, "It's time to do a process check."

— What You Can Do

This one is simple. Because you know that it's important to evaluate team processes regularly, go along with John's suggestion. There are three ways to evaluate how a team is doing. The first way, which John has suggested, is to take 5 minutes in the middle of a meeting to answer the following questions.

1. Are we on task and on schedule in terms of covering the agenda?
2. Does everyone feel that they have been heard?
3. Does anything need clarification at this point?
4. Is there anything we could do at this point to improve our process?

Taking the time to do a quick evaluation halfway through the meeting is called a process check. Process checks make it possible to correct things that are not going well during the meeting so that changes can be made right away. This prevents the team from spending time unproductively.

Bill, the group leader, says, "At the next meeting, we're scheduled to do a periodic review of how the team is doing. Take the next few minutes to fill out the checklist. Patrick has volunteered to summarize the results for us and to present the summary at the next meeting."

— What You Can Do

This one is easy, too. Go along with Bill's suggestion. Respond to the checklist as honestly as possible. The second way to ensure continuous evaluation is to do periodic reviews of team function as Bill has suggested.

The length of time between reviews will vary for each team. In general, once every 6 to 8 weeks seems reasonable. The idea is to avoid long periods of lowered productivity by making any necessary changes as soon as possible.

In Chapter 4, I introduced the High Performance Team Checklist. Every 6 to 8 weeks, all members and the leader should take a few minutes at the end of a meeting to complete the checklist. One member should be asked to organize the responses and present the results at the next meeting. The best way to organize the responses would be to determine the average response to each question and the average total response.

Begin the next meeting by going over the responses. Look at items where the average response is high (3 or 4). These are things that the team is doing well. Keep doing those things. Next look at items where the average response is low (1 or 2). Discuss strategies to improve the team's performance in those areas. Implement those strategies immediately. Don't forget to check up on yourselves. Do another evaluation about 2 months later. Repeat the process just described and make any necessary changes.

To some readers, this may seem like a waste of time. It's not. The dynamics of groups and teams can shift quickly. Before you know it, regression to earlier stages has occurred. Teams do not operate in a vacuum. Changes in the external environment can take their toll on the best teams. Budget cuts, downsizing, shifts in organizational priorities, and many other things can affect internal team functioning. Stage 4 teams are not immune to these things. They do have a better chance of surviving these pressures than groups at lower developmental levels, but only if they are vigilant.

Internal forces also can affect team dynamics. Work pressures, new members, conflicts that arise, and lots of other things can turn a silk purse into a sow's ear. Getting to the top of the developmental ladder is hard. Staying there is just as hard.

Oscar is worried that the team is not getting enough feedback about its performance from others outside the team. He says, "I think we should try to figure out ways to get better and more regular feedback from others in the organization. We get so caught up in doing the work that we don't take the time to find out what others think of the quality of that work. Can we make that an agenda item at our next meeting?"

— What You Can Do

Support Oscar's effort to get the team to discuss ways to get feedback. The third way to evaluate team effectiveness and productivity requires feedback from sources outside the team. Some teams get constant feedback about their performance. Others get almost none. All teams need to figure out ways to determine whether they are meeting goals and whether others are satisfied with their progress and output. Without feedback, it's impossible to know how to improve.

The type of feedback and methods to get that feedback will vary from team to team. The ease or difficulty of devising methods to obtain that feedback will as well. If the team's goals are concrete, it will be easier. If goals are more abstract, it will be harder. For example, if the goal of the team is to increase the number of cars produced in a quarter, feedback is easy to obtain. On the other hand, if the task of the team is to improve, or change, corporate climate, obtaining timely feedback will be more difficult. Whether difficult or hard to obtain, without feedback, the team is flying blind. Figure out ways to obtain performance feedback on a regular basis.

By the way, I included these evaluation strategies in a discussion of Stage 4 teams. Assessing group progress and obtaining performance feedback, however, is necessary at every stage of development. Do it early and often throughout the life span of your group.

Jane says, "I've been feeling a little flat at meetings for the past month. Are we getting a little dull? We were such pistols for quite a while, but I think we're starting to bore each other a little. Is there something we can do to spice things up?"

— What You Can Do

My colleagues and I have been doing research on work teams for years. One of the things that we've noticed is that teams tend to experience process losses as they age. We've noticed that after about 18 to 24 months, teams that were working at high levels start to falter. Productivity and effectiveness begin to decrease. No one is sure why this happens, but I think it may be the result of fatigue. Team members simply get tired of doing the same old things in the same old way even when those things have been effective. After all the work that goes into creating a high performance team, members tire of it. They want something new and different.

This is not surprising. Human beings tend to be a bit perverse in this regard. After years spent renovating the house, the occupants tire of the décor. After years of living somewhere, some people feel the urge to move. After months of eating a salad for lunch every day, the thought of another salad bores us to tears. We long for stability and when we achieve it, we want something different and challenging.

Teams are composed of humans, and so the urge for novelty and change influences teams. When things become too routine, most of us want a change. Our attention goes to other things and away from maintaining high levels of performance.

Again, this is as natural as can be, but, from a work perspective, it may have negative consequences. If the work of the team is completed, it might be best to disband and to distribute the now-routine tasks to others. If the work is not complete, however, team members will need to think of ways to revitalize themselves. Some ways to do this follow:

- Add additional goals and interesting tasks for the team to work on.
- Hold a retreat focused on ways to revitalize team members.
- Switch roles around so that members are doing new and different things.
- Teach each other new aspects of the work.
- Rotate some members off the team and add new members.
- Change the way the meetings are conducted.
- Change the meeting time.
- Do other creative things to energize the process.

Stage 4 is the best of times. Do whatever it takes to ensure that "the best of times" doesn't become "the good old days."

Good luck to all the teams out there. You are the real heroes of the new century. Individual heroism is a fine thing, but we need heroic teams as well. Anytime you hear of a scientific advancement, a new medicine, a school where student achievement has improved significantly, a heroic team was in back of it.

Thanks!

Bibliography

Ancona, D. G. (1987). Groups in organizations: Extending laboratory models. In C. Hendrick (Ed.), *Group and intergroup processes* (pp. 207-230). Newbury Park, CA: Sage.

Adams, J. S. (1980). Interorganizational processes and organization boundary activities. In B. Staw & L. Cummings (Eds.), *Research in organizational behavior* (Vol. 2, pp. 321-355). Greenwich, CT: JAI.

Adams, S. (1952). Effect of equalitarian atmospheres upon the performance of bomber crews. *American Psychologist, 7,* 398.

Anderson, A. B. (1975). Combined effects of interpersonal attraction and goal-path clarity on the cohesiveness of task oriented groups. *Journal of Personality and Social Psychology, 31,* 68-75.

Anderson, R. C. (1959). Learning in discussion—A review of the authoritarian-democratic studies. *Harvard Educational Review, 29,* 201-215.

Andrews, P. H. (1992). Sex and gender differences in group communication: Impact on the facilitation process. *Small Group Research, 23,* 74-94.

Aries, E. (1976). Interaction patterns and themes of male, female, and mixed groups. *Small Group Behavior, 7*(1), 7-18.

Argyle, M., Gardner, G., & Ciofi, F. (1958). Supervisory methods related to productivity, absenteeism, and labour turnover. *Human Relations, 11,* 23-40.

Armstrong, R. B., & Reigeluth, C. M. (1991). The TIP theory: Prescriptions for designing instruction for teams. *Performance Improvement Quarterly, 4*(3), 61-88.

Axelrod, R., & Hamilton, W. D. (1981). The evolution of cooperation. *Science, 211,* 1390-1396.

Back, K. W. (1951). Influence through social communication. *Journal of Abnormal and Social Psychology, 46,* 9-23.

Back, K. W., Bunker, S., & Dunnagan, C. (1972). Barriers to communication and measurement of semantic space. *Sociometry, 35,* 347-356.

Bales, R. F. (1950). *Interaction process analysis: A method for the study of small groups.* Chicago: University of Chicago Press.

Bales, R. F. (1970). *Personality and interpersonal behavior.* New York: Holt, Rinehart & Winston.

Bales, R. F., Cohen, S. P., & Williamson, S. A. (1980). *SYMLOG: A system for the multiple level observation of groups.* New York: Free Press.

Banas, P. A. (1988). Employee involvement: A sustained labor/management initiative at the Ford Motor Company. In J. P. Campbell & R. J. Campbell (Eds.), *Productivity in organizations* (pp. 388-416). San Francisco: Jossey-Bass.

Barr, S. H., & Conlon, E. J. (1994). Effects of distribution of feedback in work groups. *Academy of Management Journal, 37*(3), 641-655.

Bass, B. M. (1985). *Leadership and performance beyond expectations.* New York: Free Press.

Bassin, M. (1988). Teamwork at General Foods: New and improved. *Personnel Journal, 65*(5), 62-70.

Beckman, L. J. (1970). Effects of students' performance on teachers' and observers' attributions of causality. *Journal of Educational Psychology, 61,* 76-82.

Bennis, W., & Shepard, H. (1956). A theory of group development. *Human Relations, 9,* 415-437.

Bennis, W. G., & Nanus, B. (1985). *Leaders.* New York: Harper & Row.

Berger, J., Rosenholtz, S., & Zelditch, M. (1980). Status organizing processes. *Annual Review of Sociology, 6,* 479-508.

Berkowitz, L. (1954). Group standards, cohesiveness, and productivity. *Human Relations, 7,* 509-519.

Bion, W. (1961). *Experiences in groups.* New York: Basic Books.

Blake, R., & Mouton, J. S. (1969). *Building a dynamic corporation through grid organization development.* Reading, MA: Addison-Wesley.

Blake, R. R., & Mouton, J. S. (1964). *The managerial grid.* Houston, TX: Gulf.

Blake, R. R., & Mouton, J. S. (1978). *The new managerial grid.* Houston, TX: Gulf.

Blake, R. R., & Mouton, J. S. (1980). *The versatile manager: A grid profile.* Homewood, IL: Dow-Jones-Irwin.

Blake, R. R., & Mouton, J. S. (1982). How to choose a leadership style. *Training and Development Journal, 36,* 39-46.

Blanchard, K., & Johnson, S. (1981). *The one minute manager.* New York: Berkley Books.

Bormann, E. G. (1975). *Discussion and group methods: Theory and practices* (2nd ed.). New York: Harper & Row.

Bovard, E. W. (1951). Group structure and perception. *Journal of Abnormal and Social Psychology, 46,* 398-405.

Bovard, E. W. (1953). Conformity to social norms and attraction to the group. *Science, 118,* 598-599.

Bowers, D. G., & Seashore, S. E. (1966). Predicting organizational effectiveness with a four-factor theory of leadership. *Administrative Science Quarterly, 11,* 238-263.

Brett, J. M., & Rognes, J. K. (1986). Intergroup relations in organizations: A negotiations perspective. In P. Goodman (Ed.), *Designing effective work groups* (pp. 202-236). San Francisco: Jossey-Bass.

Brickman, P., Becker, L. J., & Castel, S. (1979). Making trust easier and harder through two forms of sequential interaction. *Journal of Personality and Social Psychology, 37,* 515-521.

Brief, A. P. (Ed.). (1984). *Productivity research in the behavioral and social sciences.* New York: Praeger.

Burke, R. J. (1970). Methods of resolving superior-subordinate conflict: The constructive use of subordinate differences and disagreements. *Organizational Behavior and Human Performance, 5,* 393-411.

Burke, W. W. (1986). Leadership as empowering others. In S. Srivasta & Associates (Eds.), *Executive power: How executives influence people and organizations* (pp. 51-77). San Francisco: Jossey-Bass.

Burns, J. M. (1978). *Leadership.* New York: Harper & Row.

Buzaglo, G., & Wheelan, S. (1999). Facilitating work team effectiveness: Case studies from Central America. *Small Group Research, 30,* 1.

Caine, B. T., & Schlenker, B. R. (1979). Role position and group performance as determinants of egotistical perceptions in cooperative groups. *Journal of Psychology, 101,* 149-156.

Callaway, M. R., Marriott, R. G., & Esser, J. K. (1985). Effects of dominance on group decision making: Toward a stress-reduction explanation of groupthink. *Journal of Personality and Social Psychology, 49,* 949-952.

Caple, R. (1978). The sequential stages of group development. *Small Group Behavior, 9,* 470-476.

Carnevale, P. J. D. (1986). Mediating disputes and decisions in organizations. In R. J. Lewicki, B. H. Sheppard, & M. H. Bazerman (Eds.), *Research on negotiation in organizations* (Vol. 1, pp. 251-269). Greenwich, CT: JAI.

Carter, L. F. (1954). Recording and evaluating the performance of individuals as members of small groups. *Personnel Psychology, 7,* 477-484.

Cartwright, D., & Zander, A. (Eds.). (1968). *Group dynamics: Research and theory* (3rd ed.). New York: Harper & Row.

Cissna, K. (1984). Phases in group development. *Small Group Behavior, 15*(1), 3-32.

Cohen, E. G. (1982). Expectation states and interracial interaction in school settings. *Annual Review of Sociology, 8,* 209-235.

Cohen, E. G., & Roper, S. (1972). Modification of interracial interaction disability: An application of status characteristics theory. *American Sociological Review, 37,* 643-655.

Conger, T. A., & Kanungo, R. N. (1988). *Charismatic leadership: The elusive factor in organizational effectiveness.* San Francisco: Jossey-Bass.

Crosbie, P. V. (1979). Effects of status inconsistency: Negative evidence from small groups. *Social Science Quarterly, 42,* 110-125.

Cummings, T. G. (1981). Designing effective work-groups. In P. C. Nystrom & W. Starbuck (Eds.), *Handbook of organizational design* (Vol. 2, pp. 250-271). Oxford, UK: Oxford University Press.

Davis, J. H. (1982). Social interaction as a combinatorial process in group decision. In H. Brandstatter, J. H. Davis, & G. Stocker-Kreichgauer (Eds.), *Group decision making* (pp. 27-58). London: Academic Press.

Deal, T. E., & Kennedy, A. A. (1982). *Corporate cultures: The rites and rituals of corporate life.* Reading, MA: Addison-Wesley.

DeMeuse, K. P., & Liebowitz, S. J. (1981). An empirical analysis of teambuilding research. *Group and Organizational Studies, 6*(3), 357-378.

Deutsch, M. (1949). An experimental study of the effect of cooperation and competition upon group process. *Human Relations, 2,* 199-231.

Deutsch, M. (1949). A theory of cooperation and competition. *Human Relations, 2,* 129-152.

Deutsch, M. (1969). Socially relevant science: Reflections on some studies of interpersonal conflict. *American Psychologist, 24,* 1076-1092.

Deutsch, M. (1973). *The resolution of social conflict.* New Haven, CT: Yale University Press.

Deutsch, M. (1985). *Distributive justice: A social-psychological perspective.* New Haven, CT: Yale University Press.

Deutsch, M. (1990a). Cooperation, conflict and justice. In S. Wheelan, E. Pepitone, & V. Abt (Eds.), *Advances in field theory* (pp. 149-164). Newbury Park, CA: Sage.

Deutsch, M. (1990b). Forms of social organization: Psychological consequences. In H. T. Himmelweit & G. Gaskell (Eds.), *Societal psychology* (pp. 157-176). Newbury Park, CA: Sage.

Dobbins, G. H., & Platz, S. J. (1986). Sex differences in leadership: How real are they? *Academy of Management Review, 11,* 118-127.

Druckman, D. (Ed.). (1977). *Negotiations.* Beverly Hills, CA: Sage.

Druckman, D. (1987). New directions for a social psychology of conflict. In D. J. D. Sandole & I. Sandole-Staroste (Eds.), *Conflict management and problem-solving: Interpersonal to international applications* (pp. 55-56). London: Frances Pinter.

Dyer, J. L. (1984). Team research and team training: A state-of-the-art review. In F. A. Muckler (Ed.), *Human factors review* (pp. 285-323). Santa Monica, CA: Human Factors Society.

Eagly, A. H. (1987). *Sex differences in social behavior: A social-role interpretation.* Hillsdale, NJ: Lawrence Erlbaum.

Eagly, A. H., & Johnson, B. T. (1991). Gender and leadership style: A meta-analysis. *Psychological Bulletin, 108,* 233-256.

Eagly, A. H., & Wood, W. (1982). Inferred sex differences in status as a determinant of gender stereotypes about social influence. *Journal of Personality and Social Psychology, 43*(5), 915-928.

Erez, M., Rim, Y., & Keider, I. (1986). The two sides of the tactics of influence: Agent vs. target. *Journal of Occupational Psychology, 59,* 25-39.

Evans, C. R., & Dion, K. L. (1991). Group cohesion and performance: A meta-analysis. *Small Group Research, 22*(2), 175-186.

Exline, R. V. (1957). Group climate as a factor in the relevance and accuracy of social perception. *Journal of Abnormal and Social Psychology, 55,* 382-388.

Fiedler, F. E. (1964). A contingency model of leadership effectiveness. In L. Berkowitz (Ed.), *Advances in experimental social psychology* (Vol. 1, pp. 149-190). New York: Academic Press.

Fiedler, F. E. (1967). *A theory of leadership effectiveness.* New York: McGraw-Hill.

Fiedler, F. E., & Garcia, J. E. (1987). *New approaches to effective leadership.* New York: John Wiley.

Fisher, B. A. (1980). *Small group decision making* (2nd ed.). New York: McGraw-Hill.

Fisher, C. D., & Gitelson, R. (1983). A meta-analysis of the correlates of role conflict and ambiguity. *Journal of Applied Psychology, 68,* 320-333.

Fisher, R. (1964). Fractionating conflict. In R. Fisher (Ed.), *International conflict and behavioral science: The Craigville papers.* New York: Basic Books.

Fleishman, E. A., & Hunt, J. G. (Eds.). (1973). *Current developments in the study of leadership.* Carbondale: Southern Illinois University Press.

Flowers, M. L. (1977). A laboratory test of some implications of Janis' groupthink hypothesis. *Journal of Personality and Social Psychology, 35*, 888-896.

Folberg, J., & Taylor, A. (1984). *Mediation: A comprehensive guide to resolving conflicts without litigation.* San Francisco: Jossey-Bass.

Forsyth, D. R., & Schlenker, B. R. (1977). Attributing the causes of group performance: Effects of performance quality, task importance, and future testing. *Journal of Personality, 45*, 220-236.

Freeze, L., & Cohen, B. P. (1973). Eliminating status generalization. *Sociometry, 36*, 177-193.

French, J. P. R., Jr., & Raven, B. (1959). The bases of social power. In D. Cartwright (Ed.), *Studies in social power* (pp. 150-167). Ann Arbor, MI: Institute for Social Research.

Freud, S. (1950). *Totem and taboo.* New York: W. W. Norton.

Friedland, N. (1976). Social influence via threats. *Journal of Experimental Social Psychology, 12*, 552-563.

Friedlander, F. (1987). The ecology of work groups. In J. Lorsch (Ed.), *Handbook of organizational behavior* (pp. 301-314). Englewood Cliffs, NJ: Prentice Hall.

Gabarro, J. J. (1987). The development of working relationships. In J. W. Lorsch (Ed.), *Handbook of organizational behavior* (pp. 172-189). Englewood Cliffs, NJ: Prentice Hall.

Galagan, P. (1986). Work teams that work. *Training and Development Journal, 11*, 33-35.

Galton, F. (1962). *Hereditary genius: An inquiry into its laws and consequences.* New York: Meridian Books. (Original work published 1869)

Geis, F. L., Brown, V., Jennings, J., & Corrado-Taylor, D. (1984). Sex versus status in sex-associated stereotypes. *Sex Roles, 11*, 771-785.

Gibb, C. A. (1969). Leadership. In E. Aronson & G. Lindzey (Eds.), *Handbook of social psychology* (pp. 205-282). Reading, MA: Addison-Wesley.

Gladstein, D., & Caldwell, D. (1985). Boundary management in new product teams. *Academy of Management Proceedings*, 161-165.

Gladstein, D. L. (1984). Groups in context: A model of task group effectiveness. *Administrative Science Quarterly, 29*, 499-517.

Glickman, A. S., Zimmer, S., Montero, R. C., Guerette, P. J., Campbell, W. J., Morgan, B., & Salas, E. (1987). *The evolution of teamwork skills: An empirical assessment with implications for training* (Tech. Rep. No. 87-016). Orlando, FL: Office of Naval Research, Human Factors Division.

Goetsch, G. G., & McFarland, D. D. (1980). Models of the distribution of acts in small discussion groups. *Social Psychology Quarterly, 43*, 173-183.

Goodacre, D. M. (1951). The use of a sociometric test as a predictor of combat unit effectiveness. *Sociometry, 14*, 148-152.

Goodman, P. S., Devadas, R., & Hughson, T. L. G. (1988). Groups and productivity: Analyzing the effectiveness of self-managing teams. In J. P. Campbell & R. J. Campbell (Eds.), *Productivity in organizations* (pp. 295-327). San Francisco: Jossey-Bass.

Greene, C. N. (1989). Cohesion and productivity in work groups. *Small Group Behavior, 20*, 70-86.

Gross, E. (1954). Primary functions of small groups. *American Journal of Sociology, 60*, 24-30.

Guzzo, R. A. (1990). Productivity research: Reviewing psychological and economic perspectives. In J. P. Campbell, R. J. Campbell, & Associates (Eds.), *Productivity in organizations* (pp. 63-81). San Francisco: Jossey-Bass.

Guzzo, R. A., & Bondy, J. S. (1983). *Guide to worker productivity experiments in the U.S., 1976-1981.* Elmsford, NY: Pergamon.

Guzzo, R. A., Jett, R. D., & Katzell, R. A. (1985). The effects of psychologically-based intervention programs on worker productivity: A meta-analysis. *Personnel Psychology, 38*, 275-291.

Hackman, J. R. (1983). *A normative model of work team effectiveness* (Tech. Rep. No. 2, Research Program on Group Effectiveness). New Haven, CT: Yale School of Organization and Management.

Hackman, J. R. (1987). The design of work teams. In J. W. Lorsch (Ed.), *Handbook of organizational behavior* (pp. 315-342). Englewood Cliffs, NJ: Prentice Hall.

Hackman, J. R. (1989). *Groups that work (and those that don't).* San Francisco: Jossey-Bass.

Hackman, J. R., Brousseau, K. R., & Weiss, J. A. (1976). The interaction of task design and group performance strategies in determining group effectiveness. *Organizational Behavior and Human Performance, 16*, 350-365.

Hackman, J. R., & Morris, C. G. (1975). Group tasks, group interaction process, and group effectiveness: A review and proposed integration. In L. Berkowitz (Ed.), *Advances in experimental social psychology* (Vol. 8, pp. 47-99). New York: Academic Press.

Hall, J., & Williams, M. S. (1970). Group dynamics training and improved decision-making. *Journal of Applied Behavioral Science, 6*(1), 39-68.

Harper, N. L., & Askling, L. R. (1980). Group communication and quality of task solution in a media production organization. *Communication Monographs, 47*, 77-100.

Hawkins, K. W. (1995). Effects of gender and communication content on leadership emergence in small task-oriented groups. *Small Group Research, 26*(2), 234-249.

Heinen, J. S., & Jacobson, E. J. (1976). A model of task group development in complex organizations and a strategy of implementation. *Academy of Management Review, 1*, 98-111.

Heller, F. A. (1969). Group feedback analysis: A method of field research. *Psychological Bulletin, 72*, 108-117.

Heller, F. A. (1970). Group feedback analysis as a change agent. *Human Relations, 23*(4), 319-333.

Hembroff, L. A. (1982). Resolving status inconsistency: An expectation states theory and test. *Social Forces, 61*, 183-205.

Hembroff, L. A., & Myers, D. E. (1984). Status characteristics: Degrees of task relevance and decision process. *Social Psychology Quarterly, 47*, 337-346.

Hemphill, J. K. (1949). *Situational factors in leadership.* Columbus: Ohio State University, Personnel Research Board.

Hensley, T. R., & Griffin, G. W. (1986). Victims of groupthink: The Kent State University Board of Trustees and the 1977 gymnasium controversy. *Journal of Conflict Resolution, 30*, 497-531.

Herek, G., Janis, I. L., & Huth, P. (1987). Decision-making during international crises: Is quality of process related to outcome? *Journal of Conflict Resolution, 31*, 203-226.

Hershey, P., & Blanchard, K. H. (1975). A situational framework for determining appropriate leader behavior. In R. N. Cassel & R. L. Heichberger (Eds.), *Leadership development: Theory and practice* (pp. 126-155). North Quincy, MA: Christopher Publishing House.

Hershey, P., & Blanchard, K. H. (1976). Leader effectiveness and adaptability description (LEAD). In J. W. Pfeiffer & J. E. Jones (Eds.), *The 1976 annual handbook for group facilitators* (Vol. 5). La Jolla, CA: University Associates.

Hershey, P., & Blanchard, K. H. (1977). *Management of organizational behavior: Utilizing human resources* (3rd ed.). Englewood Cliffs, NJ: Prentice Hall.

Hershey, P., & Blanchard, K. H. (1982). *Management of organizational behavior: Utilizing human resources* (4th ed.). Englewood Cliffs, NJ: Prentice Hall.

Hill, T. E., & Schmitt, N. (1977). Individual differences in leadership decision making. *Organizational Behavior and Human Performance, 19,* 353-367.

Hiltrop, J. M., & Rubin, J. Z. (1982). Effect of intervention mode and conflict of interest on dispute resolution. *Journal of Personality and Social Psychology, 42,* 665-672.

Hirokawa, R. Y. (1980). A comparative analysis of communication patterns within effective and ineffective decision-making groups. *Communication Monographs, 47,* 312-321.

Hirokawa, R. Y. (1984). Does consensus really result in higher quality group decisions? In G. M. Phillips & J. T. Wood (Eds.), *Emergent issues in human decision making* (pp. 40-49). Carbondale: Southern Illinois University Press.

Hoffman, L. R. (1982). Improving the problem-solving process in managerial groups. In R. A. Guzzo (Ed.), *Improving group decision making in organizations* (pp. 95-126). New York: Academic Press.

Hogan, R. (1975). Theoretical egocentrism and the problem of compliance. *American Psychologist, 30,* 533-539.

Hogan, R., Raskin, R., & Fazzini, D. (1988, October). *The dark side of charisma.* Paper presented at the Conference of Psychological Measures and Leadership, San Antonio, TX.

Hollander, E. P. (1960). Competence and conformity in the acceptance of influence. *Journal of Abnormal and Social Psychology, 61,* 365-369.

Hollander, E. P. (1978). *Leadership dynamics: A practical guide to effective relationships.* New York: Free Press/Macmillan.

Hollander, E. P. (1985). Leadership and power. In G. Lindzey & E. Aronson (Eds.), *Handbook of social psychology* (3rd ed., Vol. 2, pp. 485-537). New York: Random House.

Hollander, E. P., & Offermann, L. R. (1990). Power and leadership in organizations: Relationships in transition. *American Psychologist, 45*(2), 179-189.

Holmes, J. G., & Miller, D. T. (1976). Interpersonal conflict. In J. W. Thibaut, J. T. Spence, & R. C. Carson (Eds.), *Contemporary topics in social psychology.* Morristown, NJ: General Learning Press.

House, R. J. (1971). A path goal theory of leader effectiveness. *Administrative Science Quarterly, 16,* 321-338.

Jago, A. G. (1978). Configural cue utilization in implicit models of leadership behavior. *Organizational Behavior and Human Performance, 22,* 474-496.

Janis, I. L. (1972). *Victims of groupthink.* Boston: Houghton Mifflin.

Janis, I. L. (1982). *Victims of groupthink* (2nd ed.). Boston: Houghton Mifflin.

Janis, I. L. (1983). Groupthink. In H. H. Blumberg, A. P. Hare, V. Kent, & M. F. Davis (Eds.), *Small groups and social interaction* (Vol. 2, pp. 39-46). New York: John Wiley.

Janis, I. L. (1985). International crisis management in the nuclear age. *Applied Social Psychology Annual, 6,* 63-86.

Janis, I. L. (1989). *Crucial decisions: Leadership in policymaking and crisis management.* New York: Free Press.

Janis, I. L., & Mann, L. (1977). *Decision making: A psychological analysis of conflict, choice, and commitment.* New York: Free Press.

Johnson, M. P., & Ewens, W. (1971). Power relations and affective style as determinants of confidence in impression formation in a game situation. *Journal of Experimental Social Psychology, 7,* 98-110.

Kano, S. (1971). Task characteristics and network. *Japanese Journal of Educational Social Psychology, 10,* 55-66.

Kanter, R. M. (1981). Power, leadership, and participatory management. *Theory Into Practice, 20,* 219-224.

Kaplan, R. E. (1979). The conspicuous absence of evidence that process consultation enhances task performance. *Journal of Applied Behavioral Science, 8*(2), 346-360.

Katz, G. M. (1982). Previous conformity, status, and the rejection of the deviant. *Small Group Behavior, 13,* 403-422.

Katz, I. (1970). Experimental studies in Negro-white relationships. In L. Berkowitz (Ed.), *Advances in experimental social psychology* (Vol. 5, pp. 71-117). New York: Academic Press.

Katz, R., & Tushman, M. (1979). Communication patterns, project performance, and task characteristics: An empirical evaluation and integration in an R&D setting. *Organization Behavior and Group Performance, 23,* 139-162.

Katz, R., & Tushman, M. (1981). An investigation into the managerial roles and career paths of gatekeepers and project supervisors in a major R&D facility. *R&D Management, 11,* 103-110.

Kelley, H. H. (1979). *Personal relationships: Their structures and processes.* Hillsdale, NJ: Lawrence Erlbaum.

Kemery, E. R., Bedeian, A. G., Mossholder, K. W., & Touliatos, J. (1985). Outcomes of role stress: A multisample constructive replication. *Academy of Management Review, 28,* 363-375.

Kerr, N. L. (1982). Social transition schemes: Model, method, and applications. In H. Brandstatter, J. H. Davis, & G. Stocker-Kreichgauer (Eds.), *Group decision making* (pp. 59-79). London: Academic Press.

Kerr, N. L., & Sullaway, M. (1983). Group sex composition and member motivation. *Sex Roles, 9,* 403-417.

Kerr, S., Schriesheim, C. A., Murphy, C. J., & Stogdill, R. M. (1974). Toward a contingency theory of leadership based upon the consideration and initiating structure literature. *Organizational Behavior and Human Performance, 12,* 62-82.

Ketchum, L. (1984). How redesigned plants really work. *National Productivity Review, 3,* 246-254.

Kipnis, D. (1974). *The powerholders.* Chicago: University of Chicago Press.

Kipnis, D. (1984). The use of power in organizations and in interpersonal settings. In S. Oskamp (Ed.), *Applied social psychology annual* (Vol. 5, pp. 179-210). Beverly Hills, CA: Sage.

Kipnis, D., Castell, P. J., Gergen, M., & Mauch, D. (1976). Metamorphic effects of power. *Journal of Applied Psychology, 61,* 127-135.

Kipnis, D., Schmidt, S. M., Swaffin-Smith, C., & Wilkinson, I. (1984). Patterns of managerial influence: Shotgun managers, tacticians, and bystanders. *Organizational Dynamics, 12*(3), 58-67.

Kirchler, E., & Davis, J. H. (1986). The influence of member status differences and task type on group consensus and member position change. *Journal of Personality and Social Psychology, 51,* 83-91.

Koch, J. L. (1979). Effects of goal specificity and performance feedback to work groups on peer leadership performance and attitudes. *Human Relations, 32,* 819-840.

Kolodny, H. F., & Dresner, B. (1986). Linking arrangements and new work designs. *Organizational Dynamics, 14*(3), 33-51.

Kolodny, H. F., & Kiggundu, M. N. (1980). Towards the development of a sociotechnical systems model in woodlands mechanical harvesting. *Human Relations, 33,* 623-645.

Kriesberg, L. (1973). *The sociology of social conflicts.* Englewood Cliffs, NJ: Prentice Hall.

Kuypers, B., Davies, D., & Glaser, K. (1986). Developmental arrestations in self-analytic groups. *Small Group Behavior, 17*(3), 269-302.

Kuypers, B. C., Davies, D., & Hazewinkel, A. (1986). Developmental patterns in self-analytic groups. *Human Relations, 39,* 793-815.

Larson, C. E., & LaFasto, F. M. J. (1989). Team work: *What must go right/What can go wrong.* Newbury Park, CA: Sage.

Latane, B., Williams, K., & Harkins, S. (1979). Many hands make light the work: The causes and consequences of social loafing. *Journal of Personality and Social Psychology, 37,* 822-832.

Laughlin, P. R. (1988). Collective induction: Group performance, social combination processes, and mutual majority and minority influence. *Journal of Personality and Social Psychology, 54,* 254-267.

Leary, M. R. (1978). *Self-presentational components of leadership.* Unpublished doctoral dissertation, University of Florida, Gainesville.

Lewin, K. (1943). Forces behind food habits and methods of change. *Bulletin of the National Research Council, 108,* 35-65.

Lewin, K. (1951). *Field theory in social science* (D. Cartwright, Ed.). New York: Harper.

Lindskold, S. (1986). GRIT: Reducing distrust through carefully introduced conciliation. In S. Worchel & W. G. Austin (Eds.), *Psychology of intergroup relations* (2nd ed., pp. 305-322). Chicago: Nelson-Hall.

Lindskold, S., Han, G., & Betz, B. (1986). Essential elements of communication in GRIT strategy. *Personality and Social Psychology Bulletin, 12,* 179-186.

Locke, E. A. (1968). Toward a theory of task motivation and incentives. *Organizational Behavior and Human Performance, 3,* 157-189.

Locke, E. A., Shaw, K. N., Saari, L. M., & Latham, G. P. (1981). Goal-setting and task performance: 1969-1980. *Psychological Bulletin, 90*(1), 125-152.

Lockheed, E., & Hall, K. (1976). Conceptualizing sex as a status characteristic: Applications to leadership training strategies. *Journal of Social Issues, 32,* 111-124.

Lord, R. G., DeVader, C. L., & Alliger, G. M. (1986). A meta-analysis of the relation between personality traits and leadership perceptions: An application of validity generalization procedures. *Journal of Applied Psychology, 71,* 402-409.

Lott, A. J., & Lott, B. E. (1961). Group cohesiveness, communication level and conformity. *Journal of Abnormal and Social Psychology, 62,* 408-412.

Lundgren, D., & Knight, D. (1978). Sequential stages of development in sensitivity training groups. *Journal of Applied Behavioral Science, 14*(2), 204-222.

Lyden, F. J. (1975). Using Parson's functional analysis in the study of public organizations. *Administrative Science Quarterly, 20,* 59-69.

Mahoney, T. A. (1967). Managerial perception of organizational effectiveness. *Management Science, 14*(2B), 76-91.

Mann, R. (1966). The development of member and member-trainer relationships in self-analytic groups. *Human Relations, 19*(1), 85-115.

Manz, C. C., & Sims, H. P. (1987). Leading workers to lead themselves: The external leadership of self-managing work teams. *Administrative Science Quarterly, 32,* 106-128.

Markovsky, B., Smith, L. F., & Berger, J. (1984). Do status interventions persist? *American Sociological Review, 49,* 373-382.

Marquis, D. G., Guetzkow, H., & Heyns, R. W. (1951). A social psychological study of the decision-making conference. In H. Guetzkow (Ed.), *Groups, leadership and men* (pp. 55-67). Pittsburgh, PA: Carnegie Press.

Martin, M. W., & Sell, J. (1985). The effect of equating status characteristics on the generalization process. *Social Psychology Quarterly, 48,* 178-182.

McClelland, D. C. (1975). *Power: The inner experience.* New York: Irvington.

McClelland, D. C. (1985). How motives, skills, and values determine what people do. *American Psychologist, 40,* 812-825.

McCranie, E. W., & Kimberly, J. C. (1973). Rank inconsistency, conflicting expectations and injustice. *Sociometry, 36,* 152-176.

McGillicuddy, N. B., Pruitt, D. G., & Syna, H. (1984). Perceptions of firmness and strength in negotiation. *Personality and Social Psychology Bulletin, 10,* 402-409.

McGrath, J. E. (1984). *Groups: Interaction and performance.* Englewood Cliffs, NJ: Prentice Hall.

McGrath, J. E. (1986). Studying groups at work: Ten critical needs for theory and practice. In P. S. Goodman (Ed.), *Designing effective work groups* (pp. 362-392). San Francisco: Jossey-Bass.

McLeod, P. L., Liker, J. K., & Lobel, S. A. (1992). Process feedback in task groups: An application of goal setting. *Journal of Applied Behavioral Science, 28*(1), 15-41.

Medow, H., & Zander, A. (1965). Aspirations of group chosen by central and peripheral members. *Journal of Personality and Social Psychology, 1,* 224-228.

Meindl, J. R., Erlich, S. B., & Dukerich, J. M. (1985). The romance of leadership. *Administrative Science Quarterly, 30,* 78-102.

Michener, H. A., & Burt, M. R. (1975a). Components of "authority" as determinants of compliance. *Journal of Personality and Social Psychology, 31,* 606-614.

Michener, H. A., & Burt, M. R. (1975b). Use of social influence under varying conditions of legitimacy. *Journal of Personality and Social Psychology, 32,* 398-407.

Michener, H. A., & Lawler, E. J. (1975). The endorsement of formal leaders: An integrative model. *Journal of Personality and Social Psychology, 31,* 216-223.

Miller, C. E., Jackson, P., Mueller, J., & Schersching, C. (1987). Some social psychological effects of group decision rules. *Journal of Personality and Social Psychology, 52,* 325-332.

Miller, C. E., & Wong, J. (1986). Coalition behavior: Effects of earned versus unearned resources. *Organizational Behavior and Human Decision Processes, 38,* 257-277.

Mills, T. M. (1967). *The sociology of small groups.* Englewood Cliffs, NJ: Prentice Hall.

Mintzberg, H. (1973). *The nature of managerial work.* New York: Harper & Row.

Misumi, J. (1985). *The behavioral science of leadership.* Ann Arbor: University of Michigan Press.

Moorhead, G. (1982). Groupthink: Hypothesis in need of testing. *Group and Organization Studies, 7,* 429-444.

Moorhead, G., & Montanari, J. R. (1986). An empirical investigation of the groupthink phenomenon. *Human Relations, 39,* 399-410.

Moscovici, S. (1985). Innovation and minority influence. In S. Moscovici, G. Mugny, & E. V. Avermate (Eds.), *Perspectives on minority influence* (pp. 9-48). Cambridge, UK: Cambridge University Press.

Moscovici, S. (1985). Social influence and conformity. In G. Lindzey & E. Aronson (Eds.), *Handbook of social psychology* (3rd ed., Vol. 1, pp. 347-412). New York: Random House.

Moscovici, S. (1990). The generalized self and mass society. In H. T. Himmelweit & G. Gaskell (Eds.), *Societal psychology* (pp. 66-91). Newbury Park, CA: Sage.

Mullen, J. H. (1965). Differential leadership modes and productivity in a large organization. *Academy of Management Journal, 8,* 107-126.

Nadler, D. A. (1979). The effects of feedback on task group behaviors: A review of the experimental research. *Organizational Behavior and Human Performance, 23,* 309-338.

Nadler, D. A., Cammann, C. T., & Mirvis, P. H. (1980). Developing a feedback system for work units: Field experiment in structural change. *Journal of Applied Behavioral Science, 16*(1), 41-62.

Nicholls, J. R. (1985). A new approach to situational leadership. *Leadership and Organization Development Journal, 6*(4), 2-7.

Orkin, M. (1987). Balanced strategies for Prisoner's Dilemma. *Journal of Conflict Resolution, 31,* 186-191.

Orvis, B. B., Kelley, H. H., & Butler, D. (1976). Attributional conflict in young couples. In J. H. Harvey, W. J. Ickes, & R. E. Kidd (Eds.), *New directions in attribution research* (Vol. 1). Hillsdale, NJ: Lawrence Erlbaum.

Pennings, J. M. (1984). Productivity: Some old and new issues. In A. P. Brief (Ed.), *Productivity research in the behavioral and social sciences* (pp. 127-142). New York: Praeger.

Peters, T. J., & Waterman, R. H. (1982). *In search of excellence.* New York: Warner Books.

Pritchard, R. D., Jones, S., Roth, P., Stuebing, K., & Fkeberg, S. (1988). Effects of group feedback, goal setting, and incentives on organizational productivity. *Journal of Applied Psychology, 73*(2), 337-358.

Pritchard, R. D., & Watson, M. D. (1992). Understanding and measuring group productivity. In S. Worchel, W. Wood, & J. A. Simpson (Eds.), *Group process and productivity* (pp. 251-275). Newbury Park, CA: Sage.

Pruitt, D. G. (1981). *Negotiation behavior.* New York: Academic Press.

Pruitt, D. G. (1983). Strategic choice in negotiation. *American Behavioral Science, 27,* 167-194.

Pruitt, D. G. (1987). Creative approaches to negotiation. In D. J. D. Sandole & I. Sandole-Staroste (Eds.), *Conflict management and problem solving: Interpersonal to international applications* (pp. 62-76). London: Frances Pinter.

Pruitt, D. G., & Carnevale, P. J. D. (1982). The development of integrative agreements. In V. J. Derlega & J. Grezlak (Eds.), *Cooperative and helping behavior* (pp. 151-181). New York: Academic Press.

Pruitt, D. G., & Rubin, J. Z. (1986). *Social conflict: Escalation, stalemate and settlement.* New York: Random House.

Pugh, M. D., & Wahrman, R. (1983). Neutralizing sexism in mixed-sex groups: Do women have to be better than men? *American Journal of Sociology, 88,* 746-762.

Raven, B. H., & Rubin, J. Z. (1976). *Social psychology: People in groups.* New York: John Wiley.

Rawlins, W. K. (1984). Consensus in decision-making groups: A conceptual history. In G. M. Phillips & J. T. Wood (Eds.), *Emergent issues in human decision making* (pp. 19-39). Carbondale: Southern Illinois University Press.

Reddin, W. J. (1970). *Managerial effectiveness.* New York: McGraw-Hill.

Regan, D. T., & Totten, J. (1975). Empathy and attribution: Turning observers into actors. *Journal of Personality and Social Psychology, 32,* 850-856.

Reich, R. B. (1987). Entrepreneurship reconsidered: The team as hero. *Harvard Business Review, 65*(3), 77-83.

Ridgeway, C. L. (1982). Status in small groups: The importance of motivation. *American Sociological Review, 47,* 76-88.

Riordan, C. (1983). Sex as a general status characteristic. *Social Psychology Quarterly, 46,* 261-267.

Riordan, C., & Riggiero, J. (1980). Producing equal-status interracial interaction: A replication. *Social Psychology Quarterly, 43,* 131-136.

Rosenberg, S. W., & Wolfsfeld, G. (1977). International conflict and the problem of attribution. *Journal of Conflict Resolution, 21,* 75-103.

Ross, L. (1977). The intuitive psychologist and his shortcomings: Distortions in the attribution process. In L. Berkowitz (Ed.), *Advances in experimental social psychology* (Vol. 10). New York: Academic Press.

Rubin, J. Z. (1980). Experimental research on third-party intervention in conflict: Toward some generalizations. *Psychological Bulletin, 87,* 379-391.

Rubin, J. Z. (1983). Negotiation. *American Behavioral Science, 27,* 135-147.

Rubin, J. Z., & Brown, B. R. (1985). *The social psychology of bargaining and negotiation.* New York: Academic Press.

Sashkin, M. (1984). Participative management is an ethical imperative. *Organizational Dynamics, 12,* 4-22.

Schaible, T. D., & Jacobs, A. (1975). Feedback III: Sequence effects, enhancement of feedback acceptance and group attractiveness by manipulation of the sequence and valence of feedback. *Small Group Behavior, 6,* 151-173.

Schacter, S., Ellertson, N., McBride, D., & Gregory, D. (1951). An experimental study of cohesiveness and productivity. *Human Relations, 4,* 229-238.

Schein, E. (1980). *Organizational psychology* (3rd ed.). Englewood Cliffs, NJ: Prentice Hall.

Schein, E. (1983). The role of the founder in creating organizational culture. *Organizational Dynamics, 12,* 13-28.

Schein, E. (1985). *Organizational culture and leadership: A dynamic view.* San Francisco: Jossey-Bass.

Schein, E. (1990). Organizational culture. *American Psychologist, 45*(2), 109-119.

Schein, E. (1991). What is culture? In P. J. Frost, L. F. Moore, M. R. Louis, C. C. Lundberg, & J. Martin (Eds.), *Reframing organizational culture* (pp. 243-253). Newbury Park, CA: Sage.

Schein, E. (1995). Kurt Lewin in the classroom, in the field, and in change theory: Toward a theory of managed learning, *Systems Practice, 9*(1), 71-93.

Schlenker, B. R., Nacci, P., Helm, B., & Tedeschi, J. T. (1976). Reactions to coercive and reward power: The effects of switching influence modes on target compliance. *Sociometry, 39,* 316-323.

Schutz, W. C. (1966). *The interpersonal underworld.* Palo Alto, CA: Science and Behavior Books.

Sermat, V. (1964). Cooperative behavior in a mixed-motive game. *Journal of Social Psychology, 62,* 217-239.

Shaw, J. I., & Condelli, L. (1986). Effects of compliance outcome and basis of power on the powerholder-target relationship. *Personality and Social Psychology Bulletin, 12,* 236-246.

Shaw, M. E. (1981). *Group dynamics: The psychology of small group behavior* (3rd ed.). New York: McGraw-Hill.

Shea, G. P., & Guzzo, R. A. (1987a). Group effectiveness: What really matters? *Sloan Management Review, 3,* 25-31.

Shea, G. P., & Guzzo, R. A. (1987b). Groups as human resources. In K. M. Rowland & G. R. Ferris (Eds.), *Research in personnel and human resources management* (Vol. 5, pp. 323-256). Greenwich, CT: JAI.

Simon, H. A. (1976). *Administrative behavior: A study of decision-making processes in administrative organizations* (3rd ed.). New York: Free Press.

Slater, P. (1966). *Microcosm.* New York: John Wiley.

Smith, J. E., Carson, K. P., & Alexander, R. A. (1984). Leadership: It can make a difference. *Academy of Management Journal, 27,* 765-776.

Solomon, L. (1960). The influence of some types of power relationships and game strategies upon the development of interpersonal trust. *Journal of Abnormal and Social Psychology, 61,* 223-230.

Spradley, J. P. (1979). *The ethnographic interview.* New York: Holt, Rinehart & Winston.

Stasser, G., & Titus, W. (1985). Pooling of unshared information in group decision making: Biased information sampling during discussion. *Journal of Personality and Social Psychology, 48,* 1467-1478.

Staw, B. M., Sandelands, L. E., & Dutton, J. E. (1981). Thread-rigidity effects in organizational behavior: Multi-level analysis. *Administrative Science Quarterly, 26,* 501-524.

Steers, R. M., & Porter, L. W. (1974). The role of task-goal attributes in employee performance. *Psychological Bulletin, 81,* 434-452.

Steiner, I. D. (1972). *Group process and productivity.* New York: Academic Press.

Sternberg, R. J., & Soriano, L. J. (1984). Styles of conflict resolution. *Journal of Personality and Social Psychology, 47,* 115-126.

Stogdill, R. M. (1974). *Handbook of leadership.* New York: Free Press.

Suedfeld, P., & Tetlock, P. E. (1977). Integrative complexity of communication in international crises. *Journal of Conflict Resolution, 21,* 169-184.

Sundstrom, E., & Altman, I. (1989). Physical environments and work group effectiveness. In L. L. Cummings & B. Staw (Eds.), *Research in organizational behavior* (Vol. 11, pp. 175-209). Greenwich, CT: JAI.

Sundstrom, E., DeMeuse, K. P., & Futrell, D. (1990). Work teams: Applications and effectiveness. *American Psychologist, 45*(2), 120-133.

Swingle, P. G., & Santi, A. (1972). Communication in non-zero sum games. *Journal of Personality and Social Psychology, 23,* 54-63.

Thornton, G. C., & Byham, C. C., III. (1982). *Assessment centers and managerial performance.* New York: Academic Press.

Tubbs, M. E. (1986). Goal setting: A meta-analytic examination of the empirical evidence. *Journal of Applied Psychology, 71,* 474-483.

Tuckman, B. W. (1965). Developmental sequence in small groups. *Psychological Bulletin, 63*(6), 384-399.

Tuckman, B. W., & Jensen, M. A. C. (1977). Stages in small group development revisited. *Group and Organizational Studies, 2,* 419-427.

Vaill, P. B. (1982). The purposing of high-performing systems. *Organizational Dynamics, 11*(2), 23-39.

Van Zelst, R. H. (1952). Validation of a sociometric regrouping procedure. *Journal of Abnormal and Social Psychology, 47,* 299-301.

Vecchio, R. P. (1987). Situational leadership theory: An examination of a prescriptive theory. *Journal of Applied Psychology, 72,* 444-451.

Verdi, A. F., & Wheelan, S. (1992). Developmental patterns in same-sex and mixed-sex groups. *Small Group Research, 23*(3), 256-278.

Vinokur, A., & Burnstein, E. (1974). Effects of partially shared persuasive arguments on group-induced shifts: A group problem-solving approach. *Journal of Personality and Social Psychology, 29,* 305-315.

Vinokur, A., Burnstein, E., Sechrest, L., & Wortman, P. M. (1985). Group decision making by experts: Field study of panels evaluating medical technologies. *Journal of Personality and Social Psychology, 49,* 70-84.

Von Cranach, M. (1986). Leadership as a function of group action. In C. Graumann & S. Moscovici (Eds.), *Changing conceptions of leadership* (pp. 115-132). New York: Springer.

Vroom, V. H., & Jago, A. G. (1978). On the validity of the Vroom/Yetton model. *Journal of Applied Psychology, 63,* 151-162.

Vroom, V. H., & Yetton, P. W. (1973). *Leadership and decision making.* Pittsburgh: University of Pittsburgh Press.

Weber, M. (1946). The sociology of charismatic authority. In H. H. Gerth & C. W. Mills (Eds.), *From Max Weber: Essays in sociology* (pp. 245-252). New York: Oxford University Press.

Weick, K. E. (1980). The management of eloquence. *Executive, 6,* 18-21.

Weiss, H. W. (1984). Contributions of social psychology to productivity. In A. P. Brief (Ed.), *Productivity research in the behavioral and social sciences* (pp. 143-173). New York: Praeger.

Weldon, E., Jehn, K., & Pradhan, P. (1991). Processes that mediate the relationship between a group goal and improved group performance. *Journal of Personality and Social Psychology, 61*(4), 555-569.

Wheaton, B. (1974). Interpersonal conflict and cohesiveness in dyadic relationships. *Sociometry, 37,* 328-248.

Wheelan, S. (1990). *Facilitating training groups: A guide to leadership and verbal intervention skills.* New York: Praeger.

Wheelan, S. (1994). *Group processes: A developmental perspective.* Boston: Allyn & Bacon.

Wheelan, S. (1996). Effects of gender composition and group status differences on member perceptions of group developmental patterns, effectiveness, and productivity. *Sex Roles, 34*(9/10), 665-686.

Wheelan, S., & Abraham, M. (1993). The concept of intergroup mirroring: Reality or illusion? *Human Relations, 46*(7), 803-825.

Wheelan, S., Buzaglo, G., Tsumura, E. (1998). Developing assessment tools for cross cultural group research. *Small Group Research, 29*(3), 359-370.

Wheelan, S., & Hochberger, J. (1996). Validation studies of the Group Development Questionnaire. *Small Group Research, 27*(1), 143-170.

Wheelan, S., & Krasick, C. (1993). The emergence, transmission and acceptance of themes in a temporary organization. *Group and Organization Management, 18*(2), 237-260.

Wheelan, S., & McKeage, R. (1993). Developmental patterns in small and large groups. *Small Group Research, 24*(1), 60-83.

Wheelan, S., Murphy, D., Tsumura, E., & Fried Kline, S. (1998). Member perceptions of internal group dynamics and productivity. *Small Group Research, 29*(3), 371-393.

Wheelan, S., & Tilin, F. (1997). The relationship between faculty group effectiveness and school productivity. *Small Group Research, 30,* 1.

Wheelan, S., & Verdi, A. (1992). Differences in male and female patterns of communication in groups: A methodological artifact? *Sex Roles: A Journal of Research, 27*(1/2), 1-15.

Wheelan, S., Verdi, A., & McKeage, R. (1994). *The Group Development Observation System: Origins and applications.* Philadelphia: P. E. P. Press.

White, R. K., & Lippitt, R. (1960). *Autocracy and democracy.* New York: Harper & Row.

Wood, W. (1987). A meta-analytic review of sex differences in group performance. *Psychological Bulletin, 102,* 53-71.

Woodman, R. W., & Sherwood, J. J. (1980). Effects of team development intervention: A field experiment. *Journal of Applied Behavioral Science,* 211-227.

Worchel, S., Axsom, D., Ferris, F., Samaha, C., & Schwietzer, S. (1978). Factors determining the effect of intergroup cooperation on intergroup attraction. *Journal of Conflict Resolution, 22,* 429-439.

Worchel, S., Wood, W., & Simpson, J. A. (Eds.). (1992). *Group process and productivity.* Newbury Park, CA: Sage.

Worchel, S., & Yohai, S. M. L. (1979). The role of attribution in the experience of crowding. *Journal of Experimental Social Psychology, 15,* 91-104.

Wrong, D. H. (1979). *Power.* New York: Harper.

Wyer, R. S. (1966). Effects of incentive to perform well, group attraction and group acceptance on conformity in a judgmental task. *Journal of Personality and Social Psychology, 4,* 21-26.

Yalom, I. (1975). *The theory and practice of group psychotherapy* (2nd ed.). New York: Basic Books.

Youngs, G. A., Jr. (1986). Patterns of threat and punishment reciprocity in a conflict setting. *Journal of Personality and Social Psychology, 51,* 541-546.

Yukl, G. A. (1981). *Leadership in organizations.* Englewood Cliffs, NJ: Prentice Hall.

Zander, A. (1971). *Motives and goals in groups.* New York: Academic Press.

Zander, A. (1982). *Making groups effective.* San Francisco: Jossey-Bass.

Index

Ancona, D. G., 66
Assessment, members', 35
Autonomy, 18

Blame, 52-55
Budget cuts, 130
Buffering, 67

Charismatic leader, 74
Checklist:
    effective leader, 89-92
    effective member, 68-71
    high performance team, 47-49
    organizational support, 19-22
Coalitions, 35. *See also* Subgroups
Cohesion:
    conflict and, 64
    in high performance teams, 127
    promoting, 62-64
Collaboration, 53
Communication:

changing patterns of, 57
open structure of, 42-43, 55-57
Stage 3 group, 27
task and supportive, 58
team productivity and, 42-43
Compromise, 33-34, 65
Conflict:
    cohesion and, 64
    in high performance teams, 127-128
    limiting to tasks, 33
    personality, 107
    progress and, 32
    Stage 2 group, 25-26
    staying in, 31, 53
Conflict management:
    strategies, 64-66. *See also* Conflict
        resolution
    team productivity and, 46
Conflict resolution, 26
    leader and, 85
    methods of, 64-65
    negotiation and, 85
    success and, 112

149

About the Author

Susan A. Wheelan is President of GDQ Associates, Inc. She also is Professor of Psychological Studies and Faculty Director of the Training and Development Center at Temple University. The Center provides training and consultation to public and private sector organizations. A licensed psychologist, she has worked in a number of hospital and clinical settings. She received Temple University's Great Teacher Award in 1992.

Susan Wheelan has provided consultation to a wide variety of organizations. She has led workshops and training seminars on such topics as Executive Development, The Role of the Internal Consultation, Working in Teams, Management Skills, Communication Skills, Dealing With Difficult Employees, Leadership, Conflict Management, and many more. She has been an invited speaker in England, Ireland, Israel, the Netherlands, and the United States. Topics included group and organizational development, diversity, and conflict management. She is coeditor of *The Lewin Legacy: Field Theory in Current Practice* (1986) and *Advances in Field Theory* (1990) and is author of *Facilitating Training Groups* (1990) and *Group Processes: A Developmental Perspective* (1994). She has written more than 50 articles for publication, is currently engaged in research on group and organizational development, and is writing on these topics as well.